CHANGING THE GAME FOR
GENERATION ALPHA

CHANGING THE GAME FOR
GENERATION ALPHA

Teaching and Raising Young Children in the 21st Century

by Valora Washington, PhD, CAE

Redleaf Press®
www.redleafpress.org
800-423-8309

Published by Redleaf Press
10 Yorkton Court
St. Paul, MN 55117
www.redleafpress.org

First edition 2020
Senior editor: Melissa York
Managing editor: Douglas Schmitz
Cover design by Danielle Carnito
Interior design by Becky Daum
Typeset in Adobe Garamond Pro
Printed in the United States of America
28 27 26 25 24 23 22 21   1 2 3 4 5 6 7 8

Library of Congress Cataloging-in-Publication Data

Names: Washington, Valora, 1953- author.
Title: Changing the game for generation alpha : teaching and raising young
    children in the 21st century / Valora Washington, PhD, CAE.
Description: First edition. | St. Paul, MN : Redleaf Press, [2021] |
    Includes bibliographical references and index. | Summary: "Generation
    Alpha" applies to children born between 2011 and 2025. They will be
    raised in smaller and constantly evolving families, digital natives,
    more tech-savvy than previous generations, globally-connected, diverse,
    and will live and interact with many more generations. Because of these
    differences, the next generation and the nation is transforming in ways
    that adults have never experienced before. Valora Washington invites you
    to consider how to advocate for and influence the trajectories of this
    next generation. Raising Generation Alpha Kids looks at how this
    generation of young children presents new opportunities and challenges,
    and supports and informs the two principal groups of adults in
    children's lives-their families and early childhood educators"--
    Provided by publisher.
Identifiers: LCCN 2020040959 (print) | LCCN 2020040960 (ebook) | ISBN
    9781605547268 (paperback) | ISBN 9781605547275 (ebook)
Subjects: LCSH: Children--United States--Social conditions--21st century. |
    Child development--United States. | Early childhood education--United
    States. | Parenting--United States.
Classification: LCC HQ792.U5 W37 2021 (print) | LCC HQ792.U5 (ebook) |
    DDC 305.230973/0905--dc23
LC record available at https://lccn.loc.gov/2020040959
LC ebook record available at https://lccn.loc.gov/2020040960

Printed on acid-free paper

To J. D. Andrews

CONTENTS

Acknowledgments ix

Prologue: Let's Be Game Changers!
My Invitation to Educators and Families xi

I.   For Your Consideration: Inevitable Megatrends, Game Changers,
     and Possibilities 1
          Weigh and Consider   3
          Destiny and Decisions   4
          Choosing to Lead Our Children   6
          Alternative Futures   7
          Decades of Dialogue   9
          Change Is Not an Option; Neither Is Courage   12
          Hope, Always   17

II. Inevitable: Generation Alpha Megatrends 21
          Generations Characterize Our Lives   22
          Generation Alpha: One Generation Among Many   24
          Generation Alpha: Living in Smaller, Constantly Evolving Families   26
          Generation Alpha: Living in a Tech-Immersed Social Experiment   29
          Generation Alpha: Globally Connected   33
          Generation Alpha: Diversity Is Their Signature   35
          Generation Alpha: Transforming Adulthood   37

III. Transformative: Overview of Game Changers for 2030 and Beyond 43

IV. Transformative: Game Changer #1: Universal Systems
     for Supporting People 51
          How Our Peer Nations Support Families   53
          Pain Points Related to Limited Family Support   56
          Strategies to Achieve Game Changer #1: Universal Systems for Supporting People   59

V.   Transformative: Game Changer #2: Universal High-Quality,
     Tuition-Free Early Childhood Education 63
          Our Current State   64
          Analyzing the Gap   65
          How Our Peer Nations Do It Better   69
          Pain Points Related to Early Childhood Education   70
          Strategies to Achieve Game Changer #2: Universal High-Quality, Tuition-Free Early
          Childhood Education   75

VI. Transformative: Game Changer #3: Opportunity Equity 81
          Opportunities to Thrive in Other Nations   82
          Pain Points   84
          Strategies to Achieve Game Changer #3: Opportunity Equity   96

VII. Bold: Choosing Possible Futures 105
          Choosing Alternative Futures: Becoming Bold   106
          Archetypes and Perspectives   112
          Being Bold   116

VIII. Hopeful: Faith That We Will Do the Right Thing for
      the Alpha Generation 125
          A National Legacy of Hope   126
          A Hope Deficit?   128
          Demography: A Challenge to Hope   130
          Hope Reignited by Lessons Learned   131
          Strategies to Fill Alpha Children with Hope   134
          The Way Forward   147

Notes 153

Index 167

ACKNOWLEDGMENTS

I wish to express my appreciation to the many colleagues and family members who have shared their reflections with me on this important topic of the Alpha Generation. First of all, this book is written with warm memories of J. D. Andrews, my coeditor on two previous books about the future of young children: *The Children of 2010* and *The Children of 2020*. His insights and vision over the twenty years involved in conversations about those two works has inspired this book about the new generation of children and families.

This book focuses a great deal on what it takes to strengthen the professional and personal lives of the adults who work with young children. Acting on that commitment, for the past ten years I served as CEO of the Council for Professional Recognition where the staff and I worked to support early childhood educators. Therefore, I wish to thank the Council staff who, by administering the Child Development Associate (CDA) credential, likely touched the professional practice of early childhood educators more than any other individual professional development experience. I thank the staff who, from 2010 to 2020, realized a decade of CDA renewal, including a 25 percent increase in applications, 42 percent increases in renewals, and 107 percent decline in appeals. New initiatives included the establishment of six national conferences; The CDA Gold Standard Certification for training institutions; international programs in China, Egypt, UAE, and Panama; the launch of online application processes (which grew from 0 to almost 90 percent); new Essentials text and workbook; cyber sales; creation of the review-observe-reflect verification visit system; creation of a white paper series; high school CDA programs; renewal amnesty programs; outreach and assessments in up to twenty-three languages; and alumni group. I particularly thank Florence Murithi and Samantha Brown.

As always, another co-author with whom I've worked extensively, Brenda Gadson, has played a critical and essential role in both conceptualizing and sharing ideas in this book. Brenda and CAYL Institute program leader Ivy Wong are acknowledged with thanks.

Deep gratitude and appreciation are extended to the team at Redleaf Press who supported this work: Meredith Burks, Melissa York, Renee Hammes, and Douglas Schmitz.

Finally, I've learned so much from the millennial family members in my life, and I would like to thank Omari Washington, Kamilah Washington, Felicia Washington Dickerson, and Amera Washington.

Many thanks to all of you!

LET'S BE GAME CHANGERS!

My Invitation to Educators and Families

I was an anthropology major in college, traveling through West Africa for the summer with a team of professors and students. All I could ever think about was the children we encountered, their smiles and laughter, their usefulness in their communities, and their struggles and opportunities. And that's when the passion hit me.

That West African summer, I now realize, was a welcomed relief from the world I was experiencing back home in the United States. We Generation Boomers were coming of age in an era characterized by Vietnam War body counts, horrific civil rights abuses, a series of political assassinations, ideological competitions, and the looming drug crisis. We chose to sit in, teach-in, march on, and organize.

Issues of civil rights and justice predominated national narratives that largely focused on relationships between Blacks and Whites. And being Black from that particular era, being a "credit to my race" was a deep calling to which I answered, "Yes!" For me, "Yes!" meant service as an educator with a focus on young children. I could hardly wait to graduate from college and move on to advanced studies in child development. What could possibly matter more than helping each child develop to his or her full potential?

The science of early learning was very young back then. With theory and animal studies, we *believed* more than we *knew*. The notion of child care was controversial, but it was widely accepted that early experiences for economically disadvantaged children might help them—and our nation—win the "war on poverty." Head Start was created and along with it emerged an array of educational approaches and evaluations that revealed the necessity to take into account the racial, cultural, linguistic, and social class variations in the American context.

Very quickly, early childhood education experiences were becoming more typical for all children. Growing numbers of women in the workforce at all economic levels increased demand for child care. Kindergartens became mainstream even if not mandatory. We moved steadily from believing we could enhance children's potential to learning more about how to accomplish that with effective parenting and teaching strategies.

Now it is forty years later. I still feel that passion and excitement about advancing opportunities for young learners and supporting the educators who work with them. And now, the evidence is incontrovertible: the birth-to-age-five years are a critical period that shapes the rest of a person's life. The impact of early experience is proven to be foundational to children's social, emotional, and educational success when they are children as well as when they grow older.

If there is any one message that has emerged from decades of research and experience, it is this: the adults in the lives of children matter enormously. Parents and teachers, your interactions with children are a key factor in producing healthy, happy childhoods as well as favorable adult outcomes.

But there is another clear insight: as a nation we have moved from believing more than we know about child development to an entirely different phase. We now *know* more than we *do*. In other words, the opportunities we offer to our youngest children lag far behind the science. As a nation we have been reluctant to invest in children prior to elementary school—yet that is when the brain grows fastest and the groundwork for the future is planted. Decades of research have demonstrated that the benefits of strong parenting and effective early childhood education accrue not only to the child but to our nation as a whole.

Our inaction has consequences. Relative to comparable nations, the United States has fallen well below international norms in how well we support families and children. Parenting is a happier and deeply supported activity in some countries. Our relatively low investments result in greater infant mortality and achievement gaps that start early, becoming worse over time. As opportunity inequities mount, we see a steady diminishing of the American Dream—the hope that each generation will be better off than the previous one.

As parents and teachers, we can change this downward trajectory. Taking action matters more now than ever. The Boomer generation had a Black–White focus, but our justice and equity lens has greatly expanded. Today's young families are composed of a very diverse mix of people, languages, cultures, and experiences. Within our youngest population—the Alpha generation, or children born since 2010—children of color are a majority. Diversity is their signature! As you will read in this book, Alpha kids are profoundly different from the way we were, in very many ways that matter for parenting and teaching.

Millennial and Generation Z teachers and parents have come of age in an era characterized by relatively insecure career paths, a shaky job market, lower incomes relative to their levels of educational preparation, fewer economic supports, and a "gig" economy. Young adults today face crumbling infrastructure, climate change, inequitable educational systems, unfunded tax cuts, widening income inequality, and even terrorist attacks and pandemics. No wonder that, when polled, many of us Boomers worry about the ongoing future of the American Dream.

But together we have hope—and we are not powerless in the face of these challenges. We can be game changers.

As the seven generations now living in the United States face our future together, I welcome and invite all of us—families and early childhood educators—to join the conversation about how we can raise and teach our Alpha kids. These children are being shaped by both the legacies of who we were as well as the megatrends of who they are. Each of us must continue to do our best for the individual children in our lives. But we also have the opportunity, acting collectively, to make a difference in the lives of this unique generation.

This book will introduce you to the tech-savvy Alpha generation and then offer strategies for enhancing their lives (and the quality of life for parents and teachers too). By reviewing the megatrends in the lives of the Alpha generation, providing historical context, and shedding light on international practices, I hope you will be persuaded to take action now to change the trajectory of a generation.

With courage and imagination, we can all answer "Yes!" to the game changers that will make a difference for our children and ourselves: greater family support, effective systems of early childhood education, and opportunity equity for all. This, my friends, is the American Dream. And we create it by what we do today.

Won't you join the conversation?

Valora Washington

I

FOR YOUR CONSIDERATION
Inevitable Megatrends, Game Changers, and Possibilities

Read not to contradict and confute;
nor to believe and take for granted;
nor to find talk and discourse;
but to weigh and consider.

—*Francis Bacon*

Let's think together about our children. And let's be clear from the beginning: this brief treatise is intended to stimulate your questions about and focus on the inevitable game changers now occurring in our nation. Because of our children, our nation is transforming in ways that we adults have never experienced before. Our intention is to invite you to consider how we, as a society, want to influence the trajectories of possible futures for this next generation.

This focus on possible futures builds from the most recent work of the National Intelligence Council's framework, "Global Trends 2030: Alternative Worlds."[1] The National Intelligence Council promotes thinking about the future by differentiating megatrends—that is, patterns the future is likely to take—from game changers, or less predictable pathways.

Applying this work to young children, we begin by identifying six **inevitable megatrends** of our transforming world. The most overarching of these is the demographic shift highlighted by the emerging Generation

Alpha, our children born since the year 2010, and especially those now under age five. We contend that this megatrend is interacting with multiple variables or **transformative game changers** that will determine the kind of transformed world we will inhabit in 2030.

Based on our understanding of the megatrend and its possible interactions with the game changers, we contrast two **bold alternative scenarios** of how we—the parents, teachers, and other adults in their lives—can prepare our children for a future that we ourselves have never experienced. At one end of the spectrum is the Fixed Nation scenario in which attitudes, habits, and beliefs are so firmly established that change is very difficult, slow, or unlikely. Another alternative future is a Fluid Nation in which our national capacity to shift direction and change policy occurs more steadily and rapidly as a result of social, technological, or political forces. In the middle are many other possibilities, but the important fact is that while the demographic megatrend is inevitable, the outcomes associated with it are not. Any potential scenario will result from the choices that people make as we face expansive and widespread transformations.

In describing potential futures, my goal is to identify the opportunities and risks we face as a nation and to think about individual and collective strategies we can employ for influencing our national trajectory. As Nobel Prize laureate Dennis Gabor stated in 1963, "We cannot predict the future, but we can invent it." Gabor further stated that "All [rational thinking] can do is to map out the probability space as it appears at the present and which will be different tomorrow when one of the infinity of possible states will have materialized."[2] Obviously, we seek opportunities to influence the course of events. In the end we can always make what philosopher Daisaku Ikeda calls "the decision to hope,"[3] and to believe in our individual and collective capacity to

> "Our children are the rock on which our future will be built, our greatest asset as a nation. They will be the leaders of our country, the creators of our national wealth, those who care for and protect our people."
>
> —Nelson Mandela

accelerate the positive changes required to lead our children in the future they already inhabit.

WEIGH AND CONSIDER

Thinking about the megatrends shaping our children's lives inspires me to imagine essential game changers that could affect their lives for the better right now. Our children live in an era in which the population of the United States is aging. Luke Rogers, chief of the Population Estimates Branch at the Census Bureau, stated that more than four out of every five counties were older in 2018 than in 2010.[4] By 2034, for the first time in US history, older adults will outnumber children.[5] By 2050 people aged sixty-five and older are predicted to outnumber those younger than eighteen, a change that 56 percent of all adults say will be bad for the country[6] and for our economy.[7]

But let's dig deeper. Beyond the basic facts about the relative decline in the proportion of the child population exists another very significant megatrend: the demographic mix of our children has shifted quite dramatically. Demographer William H. Frey reports several unprecedented demographic shifts. In 2018 for the first time, non-Hispanic White residents made up less than half (49.9 percent) of the nation's population under age fifteen. The White population is aging, resulting in declines in the numbers of young Whites.[8] In contrast, mixed-race child populations have been growing faster than any other group[9] and are projected to continue growing rapidly through 2060.[10] Similarly, children of color—the combined populations of Blacks, Hispanics, Asians, multiracial, and other races—are now more than 50 percent of the under-fifteen age group. Hispanic youth comprise more than one-fourth of the children of color.[11]

But we will not have to wait to see this demographic change. In the year 2020, children of color are now the majority of the nation's 74 million children.[12] For the first time in 2014, public school enrollment of children of color exceeded that of White enrollment.[13] The population trend clearly indicates significant aging of the White population. By 2016, for the first time in our history, there were more White deaths than White births and more White seniors than White children.[14]

RACIAL AND ETHNIC PROPORTION OF CHILDREN, 2018 AND 2050 PROJECTIONS[15]		
GROUP	2018	2050 PROJECTIONS
White	50	39
Hispanic	25	31
Black	14	14
Asian	5	7
All other	5	9

Still, the overall White population is now and will continue to be sizeable. Whites as a group will be a majority of the United States population until about 2045.[16] By then, Whites will be just under 50 percent of our national population, Hispanics about 25 percent, Blacks 13 percent, Asians about 8 percent, and multiracial populations about 4 percent.[17] The Census Bureau estimates that Whites will continue to be the largest group by 2060, with about 44 percent of the US population. Whites in 2060 will outnumber the second-largest group, Hispanics, by about 67.9 million people.[18]

DESTINY AND DECISIONS

This shift in our national population is a megatrend that deserves attention. It would be better to proactively weigh and consider our responses to this megatrend than to merely notice it and leave it undiscussed. Silence about the racial dynamics of this megatrend is unlikely to be productive. The reality is that we live in a nation with a history wholly marked by racial and ethnic distinctions, discrimination, and decisions that have not always exemplified the principle from the Declaration of Independence that "we hold these truths to be self-evident, that all men are created equal."

Witness some of the impact of previous eras of rapid demographic changes in our nation. White landowners' demand for a new population of laborers forcibly transported more than four hundred thousand enslaved Africans to America during the Atlantic slave trade era throughout the seventeenth and eighteenth centuries. In the 1850s, lawmakers reacted to increased Chinese migration to the United States with legislation that limited their future immigration. White population growth in the western United States in the late nineteenth century led to the US government forcing efforts to assimilate Native Americans, including removing children from their families. Frequently marginalized since the United States purchased Alaska from Russia in 1867, the policies established during that early era set precedents for schooling practices for Alaska Natives that have resulted in misunderstandings and cultural conflicts (if the Alaskan context is acknowledged at all).

These painful memories and historical traumas resurface in contemporary society as we address population shifts, including children detained at the Mexico–United States border, population transfers, including the incarceration of a parent for one in ten African American students,[19] or population disparities, including the fact that Black and Hispanic children now represent almost two-thirds of children living in poverty.[20] These three situations highlight the urgent need our nation has to weigh and consider our responses to demographic change. Both our historic and present responses are not always in accord with our ideals of an equitable democracy.

Together we can be intentional about how we adapt to the megatrends of demographic change. Together we can create strategies that support demographic transitions in ways better aligned with our constitutional values. It's up to us to weigh and consider game changers that could potentially enhance Alpha children's lives, even if this will challenge the ways we have organized our public lives until now.

CHOOSING TO LEAD OUR CHILDREN

- Demography is a reality that is knowable.

- Our demographic destiny is unmistakable and clear.

- Our demographic megatrend is projected to continue.

Whatever perspectives you may hold regarding America's shifting population, there can be no doubt that the changes will inevitably influence our culture and our economy. Without hyperbole, we can logically anticipate that ongoing population trends and distributions will determine the future of countries, regions, and even the entire world. But the significance of what we clearly and unmistakably know is yet to be determined. Our national destiny will be written by the choices that we all make. So . . . how will we choose to lead our children?

Now is the time that we—the adults in our children's lives—must weigh and consider the choices that set the groundwork for their future, a demographic reality we have not lived through ourselves. What we cannot know, however, is the direction of the anticipated change. Exactly how will our transformed citizenry affect, and be affected by, our existing social, economic, and educational systems?

While Generation Alpha will influence and be influenced by many variables, there are several top-of-the-list game changers that will strongly determine the kind of transformed nation we inhabit in years to come. These game changers depend on the choices we make as we fill racially identifiable gaps in our current era:

> "The future depends on what you do today."
>
> —*Widely attributed to Mahatma Gandhi*

- Will we—and when or how should we—address family needs for social and economic support?

- Will we—and when or how can we—provide every child with high-quality early childhood education?

- Will we—and how quickly could we—close opportunity gaps such as those related to academic achievement or poverty?

These questions and our responses to them are the raw elements that could sow the seeds for incredible advances or social disruption . . . or some hybrid of the two. Our answers will determine the extent to which we achieve equity among our children, which we define as the elimination of racially identifiable trends in poverty, achievement, and preschool enrollment.

Unmistakably, there is considerable room for improvement in the status of all of our Alpha children, from all racial and social economic groups. As the Annie E. Casey Foundation reported in 2017, there is not one group of children that meets all of the important benchmarks of development—although there are significant disparities between groups.[21]

For decades, compared to their White and Asian peers, research has clearly indicated significant hurdles to the academic achievement of specific groups of children, notably those who are Black, Hispanic, dual-language learners, or from low-income communities. Nevertheless, reading and math skills are likely to improve as social class rises.

It becomes even more evident that race introduces biases when we notice the fact that parents' and teachers' assessments of their children (in terms of self-control, persistence, how they approach learning, and social interactions) match when broken down by social class but not by race. These racial differences in perceptions have deleterious consequences for children. For example, Patrick B. McGrady and John R. Reynolds report that studies over several decades demonstrate that, especially for White teachers, adverse assessments of a child's conduct or ability is more likely if the student is Black.[22] Further, these perceptions and stereotypes negatively affect teacher interactions with the children, which also impedes students' academic achievement.

ALTERNATIVE FUTURES

We are heading into uncharted waters, with many possibilities and perils ahead. In positing the potential interactions between the megatrends and game changers, we envision two alternative scenarios, models to stand in for the future world we are creating for our children. At one end of the spectrum is what I term a *Fixed Nation*, in which attitudes, habits, and beliefs are so firmly established that increasing social justice is very difficult, slow, or unlikely. In this scenario, inertia reigns and we continue to follow the established trajectory of our national life unless acted on by a greater force.

That greater force—the demographic reality we now face—could lead to another alternative future: a newly rebalanced Fluid Nation in which social, economic, technological, educational, and political equity becomes more widespread and less racially identifiable. Between these two extremes, of course, there are many other possibilities, but the important fact is that no outcome is inevitable. Rather, in the long term, our collective behavior and choices will ultimately decide what impact current demographic trends actually make. The choices we make individually and as a nation matter enormously.

How might you—and we collectively—respond to evolving megatrends?

What opportunities do you see as our nation grows and changes?

What unanticipated risks might we face?

What individual or collective strategies might we implement to improve the future success of your children—and our children?

None of us can foresee the future for our children. But we can reflect on, plan, prepare, and take action to create the best possible platforms from which they can launch their futures. Moreover, we hope that each of us, as the adults in our children's lives, realizes that we have individual and collective agency to take action now in our communities and homes to help bring about the future we desire.

NOW matters a lot. Our children do not live in the long term; their childhoods are *NOW*. The choices we make today play a large role in determining the outcomes we will witness tomorrow. Families and educators have power and can choose to more definitively mobilize that power on behalf of Alpha children. Will we—as teachers and families—proactively accommodate the interests of the more racially diverse populations that will lead our families, our communities, and our nation?

DECADES OF DIALOGUE

Along with several coauthors, I have been reflecting on these questions, especially those that concern children under age five, for the course of several decades. In 2000 J. D. Andrews and I coauthored *The Children of 2010*, rooted in the future-focused conversations about our nation's young children and their families taking place among early childhood educators. In 2010 Andrews and I edited *The Children of 2020*, a compendium of perspectives about the future that features many of the nation's leading thought leaders. Now, in 2020, this book, *Changing the Game for Generation Alpha: Teaching and Raising Young Children in the 21st Century*, looks at how this generation of young children, as the most diverse and tech-immersed in history, presents new opportunities and challenges for the adults in their lives. It is written in honor of Dr. Andrews, who is now deceased.

These three works together present a simple premise that could lead to profound transformations for our children and for our nation. Our children's generation points to inevitable change. We invite you to join the conversation about the potential game changers for Generation Alpha: the new considerations about rearing and teaching young children, more generous family support, and significant public investments in early childhood education that are reasonable choices to satisfy the diverse social and educational needs of Generation Alpha.

> "We are guilty of many errors and many faults, but our worst crime is abandoning the children, neglecting the fountain of life. Many of the things we need can wait. The child cannot. Right now is the time his bones are being formed, his blood is being made, and his senses are being developed. To him we cannot answer 'Tomorrow,' his name is today."
>
> —Widely attributed to Nobel Laureate Gabriela Mistral

DAY CARE, CHILD CARE, PRESCHOOL: WHAT'S IN A NAME?

In this book, we are talking about early childhood education. We recognize that many people talk about early childhood settings in many ways. Day care, child care, preschool—they are all different things, right?

In our profession, early childhood education is considered to be a distinct period of life from birth to eight years old. Yet . . .

Say *child care* or *day care* and you'll almost certainly imagine a place that keeps children safe while their parents work—but you may not picture a particularly educational setting. Moreover there might seem to be little connection between helping one person's child get quality care and serving our society at large. Meanwhile, as the thought process continues, preschool or prekindergarten is Education with a capital *E* that may yield long-term returns. The public sphere is full of media reports about the value of universal prekindergarten programs, and many communities and states are attempting to develop them. But separating "child care" from "education" is an absolutely false dichotomy given everything that we know today about the science of early learning and the importance of relationships in child development. All early childhood care matters because, for good or for ill, all of it affects the rapidly developing brains of our young children and influences their developmental trajectories.

Here are a few tips for thinking about "early childhood education" as a professional field of study for all children up to age eight:

- We know . . . the names are confusing. Early childhood education has its own complex history that has resulted in lots of program names. As a parent, look beyond labels and know that child care is not just "watching" your child but should be a high-quality learning experience even when the word "school" is not in the program label. Conversely "school" in the name does not necessarily make it a high-quality learning experience.

- Excellent early childhood education occurs in many settings. Don't confuse the setting with quality. Quality early learning programs occur in child care centers and family child care homes, in schools as well as in church basements. The location itself is not an indicator of quality.

- Excellent early childhood education occurs at all ages. It could be for a six-month-old or a seven-year-old. The content of what is being taught and learned, of course, varies across these ages. Unfortunately, many people think that staff working with infants and toddlers are "babysitters" until children are old enough to go to a "real preschool." Nothing could be further from the truth. Children are learning continuously from birth, and a skilled early educator in an infant program is doing more than changing diapers, feeding on schedule, and overseeing naps.

- Never say "day care." We cringe when we hear this term. We care for children—not days!

- Consider the needs of each child as an individual—and choose wisely.

- Learn about quality standards for early childhood education through these reputable organizations:

  - Child Care Aware: www.childcareaware.org
  - The Council for Professional Recognition: www.cdacouncil.org
  - The National Association for the Education of Young Children: www.naeyc.org
  - Zero to Three: www.zerotothree.org

CHANGE IS NOT AN OPTION; NEITHER IS COURAGE

This book aims to support and inform the two principal groups of adults in children's lives. For most children in the United States today, these adults are their families—the primary source of influence and support for Generation Alpha. Nowadays, most children are in some type of regular early childhood education arrangement—in a typical week, 12.5 million children, or 61 percent of children under age five.[23] These children are interacting with early childhood educators, a cadre of professionals who work in many settings, including family child care homes, child care centers, preschools, and schools.

This treatise is written for you—the families and educators who want to

- know more about the transformative Alpha generation;

- influence the direction of change during this significant generational shift;

- accept the bold challenge to prepare the Alphas for their future in a context that we ourselves have never experienced; and

- engage in public dialogue about how our communities and our nation might move ahead with more audacity and hope.

"Courage is the most important of all the virtues, because without courage you can't practice any other virtue consistently."

—Maya Angelou

We begin this investigation by acknowledging some critical realities about the courage it will take to lead the Alphas into the future. A tremendous amount of courage is required to do the work of parenting and teaching Generation Alpha. Many of us will indeed weigh and consider new ideas about these generational shifts for a long time before deciding on any appropriate action. We may have to reconsider our beliefs. We may have challenging conversations with our friends and colleagues. All of these steps plant seeds of growth and understanding that can deepen our sense of community in time.

But it ain't easy.

COURAGE REALITY #1: UNCERTAINTY

First, we acknowledge that many of us—as parents and educators—are often genuinely confused or unsure about how we respect our past and embrace children's futures. Generation Alpha represents an unprecedented megatrend for our nation; raising its members is surely one of the most important things a parent will ever do. It takes courage.

Wise parenting and preparation do not happen by accident, yet there is no "easy as 1-2-3" to help us do it. It would nonetheless be prudent to have both vision and practical strategies in mind as we approach our roles. Given the demographic realities the Alphas represent, what are the principles and motives that guide how we raise and educate them, when we do it, and why we do it?

There is little doubt that we teachers and parents will need to adapt to the Alpha Generation in ways that benefit them now, while they are young, as well as support their success into the future as they become teenagers and members of the workforce. Teamwork, problem-solving, and critical-thinking skills must become an even more essential part of their developmental and educational trajectories. How do we as families and teachers promote these dispositions?

> "The key to moving forward is what we do with our discomfort. We can use it as a door out—blame the messenger and disregard the message. Or we can use it as a door in by asking, why does this unsettle me? What would it mean for me if this were true?"[24]
>
> —*Robin DiAngelo*, White Fragility: Why It's So Hard for White People to Talk about Racism

COURAGE REALITY #2: EXISTENTIAL LIFE CHALLENGES

We also acknowledge that both the Alphas' Millennial parents and their early childhood educators perform their roles under less than optimal conditions. Just as children and childhood are changing, the adults in their lives are changing, too. Both primary groups of adults are experiencing more stress, and they need a great deal of courage to deal with it.

The Millennial parents of the Alpha kids face uncertainties tied to their own generational circumstances, often having greater debt, struggling with income insecurity, and finding housing less affordable than the grandparents of Alpha kids. Millennials have delayed marriage and home buying, often while living at home with their parents for longer than any generation before them. Clearly, today's young adults seem less financially independent or prosperous when compared to their parents at that stage of life. Unlike their elders, Millennials are typically earning lower incomes and facing multiple financial constraints, such as massive student debt as well as the impact of national economic factors such as the Great Recession of 2008 and the coronavirus pandemic. Millennial parents also experience both joy and distress as millions of them seek to balance their work and family commitments (an age-old but increasing challenge) and face the rising costs of child rearing.

Meanwhile, professional early childhood educators serve in an occupation that, unfortunately, has very low status and market value yet produces huge tangible short- and long-term social and economic benefits for children, families, and communities. These educators serve in a profession rife with uncertainties about its identity, expectations, and funding in an era where many Americans still do not understand the enormous talent and skill required to effectively teach young children and partner with families. These professionals too often serve within a system that undervalues and underpays them. Many are fleeing the field in record numbers, leaving child care deserts in their wake. Yet many stay and fight for change amid the deep uncertainties that dog their work.

Many early childhood educators react to the low pay and poor working conditions by leaving this field of work. The average turnover for early childhood educators is high, about 30 percent.[25] To continue teaching, many community-based early childhood educators seek employment in

UNWORTHY WAGES

Nationally, 46 percent of the early childhood education workforce qualifies for public assistance benefits. Several educators reflect on the low pay and working conditions that impact their personal and professional lives as follows:

"Early childhood education is super important, but it's really annoying how underpaid we are compared to school-age teachers. We do the same amount of work if not more and put in longer hours. . . . I have been seriously contemplating going back to school for something else, but still in the education field since this is my calling without doubt."

. . . .

"I love the job, but I can't afford to live [on] it. . . . A lot of our teachers have second incomes from second projects because it's impossible to live on these wages."

. . . .

"I do not know a single teacher who hasn't given up lunch breaks or taken work home to do into the wee hours of the morning after putting their own children to bed."[26]

In 2017 these extraordinary demands earned full-time early childhood educators a median wage ranging from $22,290 to $28,990 a year. These wages ensure that a family of four will live in poverty: in 2017 the federal poverty level for a family of that size was $24,600.[27]

public schools, but public schools often have high turnover due to dissatisfaction related to administrative support, opportunities for advancement, and working conditions. These downsides notwithstanding, public kindergartens offer higher pay and benefits than preschools, and they are attracting some of the most seasoned members of the early childhood workforce.

The coronavirus pandemic has brought national awareness to the reality that early childhood educators are essential workers. Nevertheless, low compensation leads many staff to leave the field for even modest increases. The experience of one former Colorado educator who quit the field after seven years for a job with partial health benefits and two weeks of vacation is not atypical: "People don't realize everything that goes into what we do, and I really want people to know. I want it to be important because it is," she said. "We serve this young population, and we're making it possible for like 80 percent of our population to be at work."[28]

In addition to their roles promoting child development, early childhood educators are the workforce for America's workforce. And our nation is even more prosperous because of early childhood educators: a policy brief by the Brookings Institution concluded that high-quality universal preschool could add $2 trillion to annual gross domestic product (GDP) of the United States by 2080. Although a national program would cost approximately $59 billion, it is projected to generate enough revenue to more than pay for itself.[29] The National Association for the Education of Young Children stated that in 2009, the field of early education was responsible for 1.1 percent of the GDP, or $163 billion, as much as or more than agriculture and oil and gas extraction.[30] In 2020 it was estimated that early care and education in California annually contributes $24 billion to the economic output of the state.[31]

COURAGE REALITY #3: PANDORA'S BOX

Finally, we acknowledge that many of us—as parents and educators— don't really want to talk about issues such as changing racial populations. Each of us has a racial history or recalls an incident that might seem to others to be politically incorrect. As a result, we are often reluctant to initiate in or participate in conversations that generate discomfort or strong emotions. We realize that we may have knowledge gaps or worry that the conversational context does not promote emotional safety, inclusiveness, or respect.

OPENING PANDORA'S BOX

The allusion to Pandora's box comes from the ancient Greek story about Pandora, purported to be the first human woman on Earth. She was given many physical and intellectual gifts. As a wedding present, she was given a box or jar that she was instructed not to open. Nevertheless, her curiosity led her to open the box, and misery flew out into the world. Hurriedly attempting to close the box, she locked Hope inside of it. Pandora's story ends as a mystery: what is the meaning, purpose, and impact of Hope, locked in a box? An enduring lesson from the story of Pandora is that one's actions can lead to unpredictable and undesirable outcomes. When a person tells you not to open Pandora's box, it's typically a warning: Leave the matter alone! Think twice! The consequences of your actions are unknown! Your words or behavior might cause problems! Beware!

In her book *White Fragility: Why It's So Hard for White People to Talk about Racism*, Robin DiAngelo explains the hesitance to talk about race.[32] Indeed, overcoming reluctance to talk about race, social class, gender identity, and language diversity will not be easy, but it is an essential and worthwhile pursuit because of the realities that Generation Alpha presents to us. Yes, many are weary of hearing about it. Still, the reality is that the work never stops—and it cannot stop—but we can move forward if we have the courage to deal with it head on. Racism, sexism, and other social ills in the United States have long, appalling, painful pasts that have yielded unfortunate contemporary consequences. Yes, these realities have plagued us for generations—but they don't have to be permanent.

HOPE, ALWAYS

Moving forward, raising and teaching Alpha children must become a national conversation in which we all engage. To achieve this will require empathy and compassion. We will need to recognize equity as the path to

> "Most white people consider a challenge to our racial world views as a challenge to our very identities as good, moral people. It doesn't take much—the mere suggestion that being white has meaning often triggers defensive emotions such as anger, umbrage, and hurt feelings, and behaviors such as arguing, denying, explaining, minimizing, and withdrawing. These responses work to repel the challenge, return our racial comfort, and maintain our dominance within the racial hierarchy. . . . In this way, white fragility is not weakness per se; it is a powerful means of racial control and the protection of our advantage."[33]
>
> —Robin DiAngelo

equality and encourage restorative justice. This is a participatory conversation that is vital to the well-being of the Alphas in our transformed America. Our intention is not to wallow in feelings of overwhelming despair but to inspire hope and activism. As former President Barack Obama said, "In the unlikely story that is America, there has never been anything false about hope."[34]

So, how do we act boldly in this brand-new era? What should we, the adults in the lives of Generation Alpha, actually *do*? What challenges might we anticipate? What opportunities lie ahead? The time to figure this out is now. We *can't* wait because the first five years of life are the foundation for all later learning, behavior, and health. We must be change makers ourselves while the Alpha kids are still in their most formative years.

The inevitable revolution is already here—and it is a game changer! We hope this book will spark careful thought and constructive action among all who care about our children. Let's begin our response to the revolution by taking a close look at what is, in fact, inevitable.

DEFINING THE TERMS

- **Diversity** focuses on ensuring a representation of people with different characteristics. Diversity focuses on the proportion of groups represented.

- **Inclusion**, by contrast, is deliberately creating a culture of acceptance of diversity, one in which people feel comfortable and empowered enough to participate, not just to be present.

- **Implicit bias** refers to biases that exist outside our level of conscious awareness but that are developed through the course of our lives in response to messaging, stereotyping, and experience.

- **Explicit biases** are those biases about which we have conscious awareness. Although we may try to conceal them, they nevertheless affect the perception and judgments that lead to our actions.

- **Equality** equals sameness and is not necessarily "fair." Equal treatment does not result in equal access when everybody is different or starts from a different level.

- **Equity** equals fairness. It recognizes that some individuals or groups may need more resources than others to close opportunity gaps. Equity requires more than good intentions; it encompasses the impact of processes, systems, and institutions.

- **Restorative justice** is a cooperative process that emphasizes repairing the harm caused by a behavior by encouraging all willing stakeholders to come together with the goal of transforming people, relationships, and communities.

INEVITABLE MEGATRENDS

Generation Alpha is:

1. One Generation Among Many

2. Living in Smaller, Constantly Evolving Families

3. Living in a Tech-Immersed Social Experiment

4. Globally Connected

5. Diverse

6. Transforming Adulthood

INEVITABLE

Generation Alpha Megatrends

All revolutions are impossible until they happen.
Then they become inevitable.

—*Albie Sachs*

There is a revolution taking place right before our very eyes. The revolution is in our churches, our communities, and our schools. It has even seeped into the fabric of our own homes.

Look closely: this revolution is subtle and sometimes hardly discernible. It seems low-key, like a television commercial about a common product that, without fanfare, includes a multiracial family or a few words in Spanish.

Yet the changes are obvious, an urgent invitation to a symmetrical structure of social, political, and professional relationships that enable people to recognize each other as co-equal humans. Right before our eyes, we notice movement toward what seemed unachievable for the Boomer generation: women leading the nation, Latinx culture infusing the soul of communities, multilingual music setting our feet tapping, and computers responding to our voices.

Yes, today's news is filled with challenging conversations and conflicting views on immigration, diversity, equity, race, marriage, religion, and technology. Even as this book is being drafted, data surrounding the coronavirus pandemic—a tragedy for us all—suggests that

the deadly virus is impacting Black communities disproportionately.[35] Child care staff, accustomed to being marginalized and invisible, are suddenly cast in the spotlight as essential workers amid massive closures of child care programs and families' worry about when they might reopen again. Uncomfortable realities pop up everywhere.

In both subtle and obvious ways, the revolution is public. It washes over all of us in multiple and complex situations, such as the movies we watch, the origins of our food, and the content of the daily news. Nevertheless, its impact is personal as it touches our most intimate relationships, including our hopes, dreams, and aspirations for our children. In this complicated context, increasing numbers of our children are themselves living composites of interactions between nations, languages, races, religions, and cultures.

We are now raising and educating the foreseeable revolution, one that is transformative, bold, audacious, and filled with hope. The revolution *is* our children. Who they are will change the way America is, the way we live, the voices we hear, and our choices in love.

The revolution is already identified as a cohort, the first generation entirely born in the twenty-first century and one that will inevitably embody the megatrends of our era. Generation Alpha (the generation born from 2010 through 2025) is already here. They are now babies, toddlers, preschoolers, and elementary school students. These are the children born around the same time the world welcomed the iPad and Instagram, and the word of the year was *app*.

GENERATIONS CHARACTERIZE OUR LIVES

The term *Generation Alpha* was coined by Mark McCrindle, an Australian social researcher, taking *Alpha* from the first letter of the Greek alphabet (for the first generation born entirely in the twenty-first century). Naming generations is, of course, quite arbitrary. Nevertheless, generations seemingly represent defining trends and perspectives that yield powerful (but not absolute) clues showing where to begin connecting with and influencing people of different ages. The idea of social generations not referring to family relationships was introduced in the nineteenth century. Instead of shared bloodlines, social generations tend to express comparable values

GENERATION ALPHA AND THE WORLD BY THE NUMBERS

By 2050 the United Nations' projections about population growth include the following:

- There will be 9.7 billion people in the world.

- More than half of the increase in global population by 2050 will concentrate in nine countries, including the United States.

- Populations over age 65 will be double the size of children under five and will also exceed the number of adolescents aged 15 to 24.

- The United States is projected to have 379 million people.[36]

With respect to Generation Alpha:

- 9,000 USA Generation Alpha kids are born every day.

- 2.5 million are born every week around the world.

- In 2050 (when the eldest members are forty), Generation Alpha will number 35 million in the United States and almost two billion worldwide.[37]

and inclinations through their shared cultural history, common life experiences, or factors such as age, nationality, and technology such as television. So, the concept of a "generation" is an evocative and social idea, not an absolute.

As we gaze at the horizon and peer in on the front lines of Generation Alpha, we observe many developing megatrends in their lives. They are growing and maturing in an age when life must be navigated in the face of constant and disorienting change for which there are no known answers. The point of highlighting the megatrends of this generation is to stimulate further thinking and help the adults in their lives to participate in the conversation about them.

Of course, because they are still children, much of how Generation Alpha will evolve remains to be seen. Generation-shaping trends are most influential as people come of age. Looking at people through a generational lens offers opportunities to consider potential harbingers of what we can expect from these young children.

- What context is now shaping Generation Alpha?
- Where does Generation Alpha seem to be heading?

Generational trends help inform larger conversations about education, the workforce, and our marketplaces, as well as overarching social norms. On the front lines with Generation Alpha: trends will inform how they transform the adult world ahead of them, as part of smaller, nontraditional families that have many more living generations and as tech-savvy, globally connected members of a multicultural nation.

GENERATION ALPHA: ONE GENERATION AMONG MANY

Generation Alpha will live and interact with many more generational cohorts than their grandparents, largely because of the increasing human lifespan. The global average life expectancy of humans in 1900 was 31 years; it's now 72 years. In the United States, life expectancy reached almost 79 years old in 2018, and a typical 65-year-old can expect to live to age 85.[38]

Previously people may have interacted with fewer different generations on a daily basis. The majority of the adult population in the early 1990s was in three-generation lineages.[39] Between 1998 and 2010, 40 percent of adults between ages fifty and fifty-nine were part of families with four living generations.[40] Clearly, changes in demographic situations have transformed and will continue to transform the intergenerational structure of society. Among the changes is the fact that six to seven generations are living in our country today. Consequently, it is foreseeable that over time and as adults, a larger proportion of Generation Alpha than is typical today could be part of families with four or more generations. As the Alphas mature and bring forth their own worldviews (many of which will build upon that of previous generations), they will benefit from exposure to many more perspectives and learn the diverse ways that various generations think and approach problem solving.

Nevertheless, the interplay of generations is not without challenges, chiefly the perceived competition for economic security across generations. Even now we see young adult cohorts bewildered—and even angry sometimes—about the dwindling odds of achieving the American Dream compared to their elders. Previous generations, specifically the Boomers (who in many cases are their parents), are a prime target for blame. Some Millennials worry that, rather than turning their roles over to the next generation, their elders have left them with insecure career paths, a shaky job market, lower incomes relative to their levels of educational preparation, fewer economic supports, and a "gig economy"—concerns with some basis in fact. Indeed, Boomers are redefining and postponing retirement because many of them do not consider full retirement a smart or healthy option.

Bruce Cannon Gibney discusses this generational dilemma with both directness and a dry sense of wit in his book *A Generation of Sociopaths: How the Baby Boomers Betrayed America.* His essential point is that by indulging themselves, assuring their own prosperity and refusing to make fairly minimal sacrifices, Boomers leave their children the daunting tasks of handling crumbling infrastructure, climate change, and inequitable educational systems. He writes, "Because the problems Boomers created,

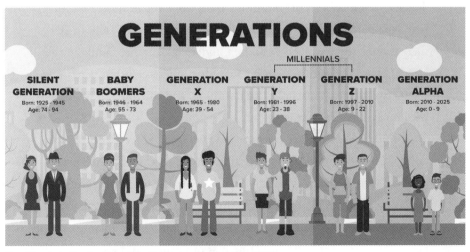

Graphic created by the Council for Professional Recognition, 2020

from entitlements on, grow not so much in linear as exponential terms, the crisis that feels distant today will, when it comes, seem to have arrived overnight."[41] In his review of Gibney's book, Ben Schieller writes, "The boomers have satisfied their needs by squandering our inheritance. They've passed unfunded tax cuts that we'll be paying off for years. They've protected Social Security checks while leaving us with trillions in student debts. They've waged NIMBY [Not In My Backyard] campaigns against new housing while protecting the value of their condos."[42] Of course, there are solutions and sources of hope, as Gibney points out, and they'll become increasingly important as several generations continue to live and work together.

GENERATION ALPHA: LIVING IN SMALLER, CONSTANTLY EVOLVING FAMILIES

While the number of generations living may be increasing, the number of children in each family is shrinking. And the families in which they live have growing complexity and diversity.

THE ALPHA GENERATION CHILDREN WILL LIVE IN SMALLER FAMILIES

These Generation Alpha offspring will more likely be only children, as one-child families continue to gain ground. Researchers for data platform Statista published a report indicating that, while the number of families with any children has stayed more or less constant since 2000, in 2019 there was an average of 1.93 children under eighteen per family in the United States, a decrease from 2.33 children under eighteen per family in 1960. Two-parent households are declining, and the number of families with no children is increasing.[43]

Family size preference has changed over time. Since 1971, the ideal family size has dropped from four kids to two, reflecting a clear preference for a smaller family. These preferences are the result of many factors, including advances in ability to control fertility, increased employment among women, the rising cost of living that requires two incomes to support a household, and the escalating cost of raising children.[44]

Finances and the economy are important considerations when individuals consider having children. A family's size and structure play vital roles in its financial success; studies of intergenerational economic mobility have clearly indicated that typical families in the United States can no longer expect that one earner in a household will create a pathway for upward mobility.[45] Therefore it is not surprising that, in 2013, when Gallup asked why couples weren't having more kids, 65 percent of Americans, with or without children, cited the expense of raising children.[46]

Without question, raising Generation Alpha will require significant financial resources. Parents spend between 9 and 22 percent of their total income on children at a cost that has risen from $198,560 in 1960 (adjusted for inflation)[47] to about $233,610 for a child born in 2015.[48] After excluding college expenses, the largest costs were housing, childcare/education and food. According to data from the US Department of Agriculture, which regularly tracks the price tag attached to raising a child, the average family "will spend approximately $12,980 annually per child in a middle-income (with an income of $59,200–$107,400), two-child, married-couple family."[49]

The costs of raising children and changing social attitudes together yield noteworthy effects on the Alpha generation: declining family size means that Alpha kids will be a smaller proportion of the total population of the future United States. There has been a steady decrease in the percentage of children: 36 percent in 1960, 26 percent in 1990, and 24 percent in 2010, with estimates of 20 percent by 2050.[50]

CHANGING VIEWS ABOUT ONLY CHILDREN

"Being an only child is a disease in itself."

—Renowned child psychologist Granville Stanley Hall, A Study of Peculiar and Exceptional Children, 1897

"Today only-child families are a given and rapidly becoming the New Traditional Family."

—Social psychologist Susan Newman, The Case for the Only Child: Your Essential Guide, 2011

THE ALPHA GENERATION CAN EXPECT TO LIVE IN MORE VARIED FAMILY COMPOSITIONS THAN THEIR ELDERS DID

A 2015 series of Pew Research Center investigations into the American family clearly indicate the future of the family for Alpha children. Not only will Generation Alpha be demographically different from previous generations, but their families will different as well. Their parents will be more likely be unmarried, older by about five years (twenty-six versus twenty-one years old in 1970), and have a higher education.[51]

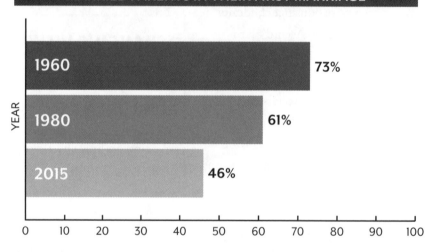

PERCENTAGE OF CHILDREN LIVING IN A FAMILY WITH TWO MARRIED PARENTS IN THEIR FIRST MARRIAGE

GROUP	PERCENTAGE OF CHILDREN LIVING IN A FAMILY WITH TWO MARRIED PARENTS IN THEIR FIRST MARRIAGE
Asian	71
White	52
Hispanic	43
Black	22

Source: Pew Research Center, 2015[52]

Generation Alpha will be reared in a nation that does not have a dominant family form. The diversity of family types is a result of the overall drop in fertility, smaller families, a decline in two-parent households, and the rise of single-parent families, blended families, and multiple-partner fertility.

The rise in single parent families includes a growing share of children who live with a single dad. Examining all US households, the Pew Research Center reported a ninefold increase in those comprised of a single dad, from about 1 percent of all US households in 1960 to about 8 percent in 2011.[53]

Moreover, the Alphas' families will be fluid. The Pew Research Center analysis points out that the family structures in which children live will continue to change throughout children's lives for several reasons, including nonmarital cohabitation, divorce, remarriage, or death. Indeed, one study found that about one-third of children younger than six had experienced a major family change for one of those reasons.[54]

Cohabitation of unmarried adults plays an important role in the family structures that children experience. By the time they are twelve, almost 40 percent of children will have had a mother in a cohabiting relationship, a rate that increases to almost half by the time they are sixteen. Just as divorce became more typical in an earlier era, fluid family structures may become normalized for the Alpha generation. Indeed, the proportion of younger adults with stepsiblings is increasing as blended families become more common.[55]

GENERATION ALPHA: LIVING IN A TECH-IMMERSED SOCIAL EXPERIMENT

In all types of families, Generation Alpha's engagement with technology is unparalleled, even when compared to their parents, who often are themselves digital natives. Technology is infused into the Alphas' young lives by parents who are quite comfortable with digital innovations and who are preparing their children for a life online—sometimes even before they are born. Having a digital presence is not just a phenomenon among celebrities. According to data from GoDaddy, a web hosting company, nearly half of Millennial parents believe it is important for their children to have an online presence early in life and engage in activities such as establishing social media accounts, creating websites for the children that can grow with them into adulthood, and even changing a baby's name based on the availability of that domain name.[56]

Often Millennial parents are quite comfortable connecting their young children to innovative technology tools, such as health wearables, artificial intelligence (AI) diagnoses and treatments, or robot surgeons. A recent study from the Institute of Electrical and Electronics Engineers (IEEE) notes that 40 percent of Millennial parents are open to replacing or supplementing a human nanny with a robot, and about three-quarters would think about an AI tutor.[59] Even for Millennials and Gen Z, technology may still be a tool. For Alphas, it's the way life is.

With technology infused into their lives since infancy, the members of Generation Alpha don't know or cannot imagine how to live without it. Young Alpha children are intrigued by—not afraid of—the technology and enjoy exploring it to see what the buttons and screens can do. Not surprisingly, more than 80 percent of parents report that their children under age six watch videos or use electronic devices every day.

Although about one third of parents feel that too much time is spent on these activities, two-thirds are comfortable with the amount of time their children spend on these activities.[61]

Generation Alpha children are growing up with familiar and user friendly conversational technology such as Siri, Alexa, and Google Assistant in their homes. In the world of the Alphas, interacting with AI and voice assistants is simply normal and natural. These kids often assume that a device is touchscreen until proven otherwise. Because of this, Alphas are considered both the Glass Generation, due to the dominance of their glass-fronted devices, and Generation Voice, due to their use of voice assistants.

What is the impact of all this technology on child development and learning? Exactly how soon should children be exposed to it? And how much is enough—or too much? The American Academy of Pediatrics recommends

TECHNOLOGY IMPACTS CREATIVE PLAY?

"Years ago, if you gave a child a lump of Play-Doh, she might roll it around in her hands and shape it into a ball, a lion, or some other figment of her imagination. These days children are more likely to look at that lump, scratch their heads and ask, 'What does it do?'"[60]

—Diane Levin, professor, Boston University Wheelock College of Education and Human Development

- Under eighteen months: avoid screen media other than video chatting.

- Eighteen to twenty-four months: select and watch high-quality programming with children.

- Two to five years: keep media use under one hour per day of high-quality programs.[62]

> "Not only has screen time been linked to language delay and smaller vocabularies, but studies show that the more television infants and toddlers are exposed to, the more likely they are to be inactive and obese, have difficulty sleeping, and show aggression . . . . Very young children learn best by relating to real live people, but they also learn by moving and doing."[63]
>
> —*National Center for Health Research*

Ashley Fell, the communications director for the research company McCrindle, told *Good Morning America* that Alpha children are "part of an unintentional global experiment where screens are placed in front of them from the youngest age."[64] Consequently, they may have diminished proficiency in practical skills, assessing and approaching risk, and setting and achieving goals.

Whatever the risks or benefits of this wide-scale social experiment, it is very clear that Alpha kids are very open to technology. Many of these children, members of smaller families, own their own devices and therefore have no need to practice sharing resources or negotiating their use with others (remember when families had one TV in the home?) Who has not witnessed the hysterical response of young children losing control when an adult takes away their devices? One child summed up the Alphas' feelings by saying, "I'd rather have an iPad— better than a dog."[65]

Commercial interests know the connected Alphas are already a lucrative consumer market. Their influence on their parents' buying decisions is already huge since Alpha parents are willing to spend a lot on their children. And, in the future, this impact could grow. For example, as tech companies develop greater capacity to personalize their functions, they could use voice assistants to create loyal, lifelong relationships with Alpha consumers. Eric Turkington, a voice strategy, design, and development expert, imagines that as highly personalized and individualized voice assistants become socially acceptable, opting out of these personalized experiences can become a significant obstacle to being a part of modern society. An important question then becomes "Who owns the data?"

GENERATION ALPHA: GLOBALLY CONNECTED

For Generation Alpha, technology helps open doors to the world, creating similarities across generations around the globe. Typically, social and cultural generations, as

> "If Generation Alpha possesses similar behaviors, attitudes and beliefs to that of their parents, then to win a certain segment of Millennial consumers (Millennial parents), we must target Generation Alpha."[66]
>
> —*Google marketers, as quoted in* Forbes

well as designated generational birth years, may be different around the world due to unique cultural, political, and economic influences. For example, a Millennial in a nation dominated by civil unrest is likely to have different expectations and behaviors than a Millennial born in a stable democracy.

Millennials, generally the Alphas' parents, were the first generation to help collapse the international divide across generations. And Generation Alpha will certainly inherit a world in which global issues are likely to be front and center in their personal and political lives.

Generation Alpha will be very much shaped by shifts in global power that have been underway since the first of them was born in 2010. They are witness to the rising might of large emerging economies, such as China, India, Russia, and Brazil. Another consideration for the shifts in global power is the demographic imbalance in the world. Although the United States may have a smaller child population than in the past, the world in general may be more demographically lopsided: older adults may comprise a greater proportion of the population in relatively wealthy countries and the young in relatively poorer nations, and some countries will have high fertility and rapid population growth while other nations face decreasing population due to low fertility or emigration.

As Somini Sengupta, a United Nations correspondent, explains, "The world has a problem: Too many young people."[67] She warns of potentially dire consequences: disrupted global economies, political unrest, and mass migration, to name a few. The Alpha children will certainly be affected by these circumstances.

It is unlikely that Generation Alpha will be shaped by an era of unprecedented demonstration of American exceptionalism like their grandparents and great-grandparents. We already see generational divides in how Americans view our nation. A Pew Research Center report from the start of 2020 (before the COVID-19 pandemic) found that 79 percent of adults believe the United States is either the best or else among the greatest countries in the world. However, while 21 percent of all adults say other countries are better, this number jumps among young adults (age eighteen to twenty-nine), 36 percent of whom agree with the statement.[68] Negative perception of the country's response to COVID-19 may affect this assessment into the future, too.[69]

What might Alpha children believe? By the late 2020s, while the Alphas are still children, some forecasts suggest the size of China's economy might surpass that of the United States. Without doubt, Generation Alpha will inherit,

AMERICAN EXCEPTIONALISM DEFINED

"American exceptionalism is not the same as saying the United States is 'different' from other countries. It doesn't just mean that the US is 'unique.' . . . Exceptionalism requires something far more: a belief that the US follows a path of history different from the laws or norms that govern other countries. . . . The US is not just a bigger and more powerful country—but an exception. It is the bearer of freedom and liberty, and morally superior to something called 'Europe.'"[70]

—Ian Tyrrell, emeritus professor of history, University of New South Wales, Australia grow up in, and have to navigate a new normal as our nation may play a different role on the world stage. Indeed, best-selling author Yuval Noah Harari notes that three world challenges, "nuclear war, ecological collapse and technological disruption—threaten the future of human civilization if the world remains divided among rival nations"[71] and if we refuse to cooperate on a global scale.

GENERATION ALPHA: DIVERSITY IS THEIR SIGNATURE

As it faces global issues, the US Alpha population itself is the most strikingly diverse generation in our history. Diversity is the new normal and likely irreversible. Even by 2018, the White median age of almost forty-four was much higher than that of Latinx or multiracial residents (almost thirty and just over twenty, respectively).[72] Rising numbers of children of color are emerging as the White population ages and grows slowly.

Clearly, racial and ethnic minorities are the primary demographic engines of our nation's future growth:

- **Ethnic blending will continue.** The share of mixed-race children is set to double, and the largest growth rates are projected for multiracial populations.

- **Children of color are the fast-growing populations, especially Hispanics and Asians.** Even when one considers changes in census questions or personal heritage selections, proportions of the US child population at a minimum approximate less than 50 percent White, 26 percent Hispanic, 14 to 15 percent Black, 5 percent for Asian and Pacific Islanders, 4 percent mixed race, and 1 percent American Indians or Alaska Natives.[73]

- **Immigration matters.** The Pew Research Center reports that immigration is the major factor that explains the substantial increase in Hispanic and Asian populations in the United States. The impact of immigration has been particularly significant since 1965, when the visa system that favored Europeans ended. Between 1965 and 2015, immigration accounted for the most growth in the Hispanic population (76 percent) and virtually all growth in the Asian population (98 percent).[74]

- **Each generation is more racially diverse.** The share of the White population is 70 percent or more for Boomers and earlier generations; 59.7 percent for Gen X; 55.1 percent for Millennials; and less than 50 percent for Gen Z and Generation Alpha.[75]

- **The demographics of people of color are changing too.** In 1965 the nation was about 84 percent White. Blacks, at 11 percent of the population, were the dominant minority group. Then, Hispanics were about 4 percent of the population and all other races comprised the remaining 1 percent.[76] Now, Hispanics are the largest group of people of color for Generation Alpha, Millennials, and Gen Z.[77] In the decades since 1965, the Hispanic proportion of the population quadrupled, the Asian portion quintupled, the White portion declined, and the Black portion remained stable.[78]

The impact of this national diversity may not be felt by all regions simultaneously. William Frey's analysis for Brookings demonstrates that although child diversity is spreading, the pattern of diversity has not spread evenly across all states:

- **Twenty-eight states have losses in the number of children in their communities.** This is because the declining number of White children is not countered by gains in other cultural groups.

- **Already the under-fifteen population in fourteen states plus the District of Columbia is minority White.** The list includes populous states like California, Texas, Florida, and New York. In the birth to age four population, White children are also minorities in these fourteen states and also in Louisiana.

- **Metropolitan areas will change composition.** The under-age-fifteen populations already are minority White in forty-two of the nation's one hundred largest metropolitan areas.

- **County demographics are changing too.** In 672 of the 3,141 counties in the nation, the under-fifteen population is minority White.[79]

WHAT WILL COLOR—OR RACE—MEAN TO THE DIVERSE GENERATION ALPHA?

Despite both biographical and DNA evidence about extensive mixed racial ancestry within US populations, race and identity are socially constructed, transmitted across generations, and often imposed by political, economic, and social sanctions tied to legal or institutional behavior. Because race is a social and not a biological construct, the boundaries of race and ethnicity have been fluid for some individuals or groups, allowing for once-excluded others to "become White" by social consensus or personal choice. Historic racism has motivated many to minimize or negate non-White ancestries and to assimilate into White American culture if possible as a result of light skin color, altering surnames, or changing cuisine preferences.

Will this pattern of preference or absorption into a White identity continue in the twenty-first century? As identity is now classified, the United States will have a multicultural majority and be minority White by 2045—a status that already exists within Generation Alpha. Moreover, many ethnic or racial groups sustain deep pride in their heritages and have no desire to dissolve into the metaphorical racial melting pot—or to even be tossed into a metaphorical salad bowl.

Will increases in multiracial Generation Alpha children blur racial group boundaries? Will our nation's political, social, and economic behavior reinforce racial group solidarity and hierarchies? How will race and ethnicity affect the chosen identities of Alphas as they become adults?

GENERATION ALPHA: TRANSFORMING ADULTHOOD

Several futurists and demographers—Mark McCrindle and Ashley Fell are leaders among them—predict that as Alphas become adults, they may make up the longest-lived and wealthiest generation that the world has witnessed. Trends in demographics show that as racially diverse younger generations become working, tax-paying consumers and entrepreneurs,

CONTRASTS IN DRAWING THE COLOR LINE

"The problem of the twentieth century is the problem of the color line."

—W. E. B. DuBois, 1903

"One of the common features of whites and blacks is their preference for a single-race identity. . . . Blacks and whites are generally unwilling to acknowledge multiracial ancestry. . . . Nearly half of all Hispanics are unwilling to identify with a single standard race . . . many Hispanics do not identify themselves with the standard categories of American racial statistics and see little need to report an identity beyond their Hispanic/Latino origin."[80]

—US Census analysis, 2009

It seems that some things haven't changed: W. E. B. DuBois's 1903 statement agrees with recent census data, and both Blacks and Whites draw a relatively strong line between the races. But in contrast, the Latinx population seems to find race more fluid or shows greater recognition that Hispanic heritage includes multiple races. What will color or race mean to the Alpha generation as time moves forward?

their unique interests and inclinations will shape our systems of employment, social security, retirement, and education.

BETTER AND DIFFERENTLY EDUCATED

As the initial responses to the coronavirus make evident, education may be revolutionized for the Alpha Generation. With more highly prized online and nontraditional certification options at every stage of development, traditional educational institutions will need to reinvent and demonstrate value while reducing their debt burdens, if they wish to engage Alphas.

Lifelong learning will characterize the Alphas' educational experience. They will typically begin schooling in early childhood and find that continuing education will be a womb-to-tomb necessity for them. Degree programs could become largely obsolete as a result of automation, machine learning, and artificial intelligence, as many new pathways to demonstrate competency are created. Meanwhile, corporate sponsors will be eager to tap into talent before graduation day. Indeed, the very meaning of "graduation" may diminish as lifelong and more specialized learning becomes more typical and retraining becomes even more essential.

A GENERATION OF SPECIALISTS

It is not a new notion to predict that, like their generational predecessors, Generation Alpha is likely to be employed in many jobs and sectors that do not currently exist. But there are additional complexities:

- To what extent will employment be more widely and fundamentally disrupted by automation?
- How will these potential disruptions change the

"The key to a workforce development program is that a company is able to find the right people with the right skills at the right time. With people, it's a combination of quality, capabilities, and diversity. . . . Employers are increasingly finding themselves in the "post and pray" mode. . . . The big challenge we have as a country is that we haven't built out the social infrastructure, where there's a constant sequence of skilling, reskilling, and upskilling. The challenge for us is figuring out how to set up the systems so that the on-ramp and off-ramp to training, employment, and reskilling is more fluid, rather than just early [in high school and college] and once in a lifetime."[81]

—*Van Ton-Quinlivan, executive at Pacific Gas & Electric who built workforce development programs* meaning of employment or the educational requirements for any specific job role?

- Will the future for less-trained workers be dominated by low-paying service jobs that cannot yet be automated?

Many observers of Generation Alpha anticipate that its members will need to develop highly specialized technical skills in order to find and sustain fulfilling work. As a result of technological advances, Generation Alpha will require continuing education, constant retraining, or increasingly specialized training multiple times over their lives. Another potential outcome is a deepening divide between the rich and poor if an elite group of individuals gets the support to attain highly specialized roles while others are left without meaningful work.

A GENERATION OF ENTREPRENEURS

As career pathways become less predictable or stable, by both necessity and temperament, Generation Alpha will be a more entrepreneurial generation. Their early and sustained access to information, people, and resources may make them better prepared for the already widespread freelance economy that even by 2018 included 35 percent of workers in the United States.[82] In order to have more prosperous lives, Generation Alpha will require that the nation engage and retain autonomous and mobile employees or contractors with greater attention to equity, flexibility, working conditions, and legal protections.

CREATING BALANCE AND BOUNDARIES

Given rapid changes in education and employment, Generation Alpha as adults will be required to consider new and different issues related to work-life balance and boundaries. Alphas will be expected to change jobs more frequently, often on freelance contracts, as the commoditization of labor increases and robots begin to take over more production. This fast-paced and flexible approach to work is revolutionary—and potentially jarring to the psyche. Historian Yuval Noah Harari worries that the rise of AI might eliminate the economic value and political power of most humans, making many of them essentially useless. How do we protect people, if not jobs, in this era? Should income be subsidized? Should basic needs and services be universally provided without costs? As Harari states, "In order to cope with the unprecedented technological and economic disruptions of the twenty-first century, we need to develop new social and economic models as soon as possible."[83] Notably, the United States lacks a social safety net for this type of employment scenario.

> "It is far from clear that billions of people would be able to repeatedly reinvent themselves without losing their mental balance."[84]
>
> —Yuval Noah Harari, historian

THE ECONOMIC FOUNDATION OF OUR NATION

Along with the financial demands of supporting new employment models, there will be a boom in aging populations just as Generation Alpha is reaching adulthood and moving towards their greatest earning potential. Alphas will ultimately support health care, social care, and retirement systems for a larger number of elderly people in society as a whole. Calls for racial justice in matters such as employment and income, including the Black Lives Matter movement, will intensify in the face of ongoing inequity as demographic change takes root.

How will Generation Alpha fare as the economic foundation of our nation, responsible for their own young and the elderly while balancing new work-life demands with a legacy of social and racial inequality? How might Generation Alpha serve as a bridge to greater social equality? What can we—the adults in their lives right now—do today to start preparing Generation Alpha for tomorrow?

> "All wealth and power might be concentrated in the hands of a tiny elite, while most people will suffer not from exploitation but from something far worse—irrelevance."[85]
>
> —Yuval Noah Harari

TRANSFORMATIVE GAME CHANGERS

- Game changer #1: Systems for supporting people, including paid family leave and greater visibility for unpaid work, must become universal.

- Game changer #2: High-quality, tuition-free early childhood education should be available for all children.

- Game change #3: Equity of opportunity for all Alpha children needs to become a unifying objective for family empowerment and mobilization.

TRANSFORMATIVE

Overview of Game Changers for 2030 and Beyond

You will teach them to fly, but they will not fly your flight.
You will teach them to dream, but they will not dream your dream.
You will teach them to live, but they will not live your life.
Nevertheless, in every flight, in every life, in every dream,
the print of the way you taught will always remain.

—Typically attributed to Mother Teresa

Teaching Generation Alpha to fly is no small matter for the adults in their lives. Raised by tech-savvy Millennial parents, immersed in technology from birth, bombarded by advertising, and growing up in an era where diversity is the norm, this generation is the first to be entirely born in the twenty-first century. They are also likely to be the age group that inspires deep reconsiderations of both parenting and early childhood education because of who they are. Indeed, as a result of the changes we anticipate from this new Alpha generation, we, as citizens and adults, can make transformative choices in how we view our roles as parents, teachers, and members of a people-centric society.

We often teach Generation Alpha to dream when we ourselves are sleep-deprived! We are awake and untangling a thorny knot of competing demands for parental attention. One-third of us *always* feel rushed, and half of us *sometimes* feel

rushed—sentiments that make parenting tiring, stressful, and less en-
joyable. High-income parents in particular believe that their children's
schedules are too hectic.[86]

With parents' stressed-out, multitasking lives, who has time to
transform the American childhood for Generation Alpha? Parenthood
isn't child's play, and big-picture thinking about what we are doing as
parents can often take a back seat to daily responsibilities. The routines of
feeding, sleeping, pottying, and cleaning can challenge the most composed parent—not to mention worries about sleepless nights, sibling
fights, academic demands, challenging behavior, bullying, social media,
school shootings, and the perfection pressures of "mommy blogs." Some
families have angst about whether to work or stay home with their kids
(if they have the privilege of that choice in the first place), feel guilty or
unhappy for working, or feel judged by others even if they are happy with
their choice. For some parents, worries include unsafe neighborhoods or
community violence. And as this book goes into production, families are
balancing the need to work and homeschool their children in the midst
of a coronavirus pandemic that has quarantined many families in their
homes. Some of these issues reflect our current era (social media and the
pandemic), but others (challenging behavior) are perennial. How can
anyone be prepared for all the pressures and anxieties that emerge in the
early years of parenting?

Peek into family life and we often see that very young children, their
older siblings, and the adults in their lives spend increasing amounts of
time with various technological devices. The National Recreation and
Park Association reported that children today are spending seven minutes
or less in unstructured outdoor play but seven-and-a-half hours in front
of electronic media—a dramatic change from previous generations.[87]
Many families, as well as the public at large, perceive risk in daily life
circumstances. What once seemed to be a typical free-roaming childhood
is today considered socially and sometimes legally an insufficient level of
supervision.

A Pew Research Center study provides indicators of parental beliefs
about supervision of children today. Children should be at least ten years
old to play outside unsupervised (in front of the house with an adult at

home inside); twelve to stay home alone for an hour, and fourteen to go to the park alone.[88]

Given these expectations, there is little wonder why adult-planned activities and helicopter parenting styles appear predominant in child life today. Forty percent of young children under six have played sports or attended a play group. One-third of parents report that their young children have taken lessons such as music, dance, or art.[89]

Just as parenting young children is changing, their education is changing, too. Teaching young children today requires enormous knowledge and skill. The notion that early childhood educators "play with kids all day" is a stereotype that even the briefest visit to a program would quickly dispel. The most effective early childhood educators are masters of intentionality and skilled observers whose work results in powerful interactions with children. Today's multilingual early childhood education settings—in many programs across the nation, not just in urban areas—represent a Tower of Babel where educators interact with familial and cultural diversity in tandem with helping children regulate their emotional responses, express empathy, and deal with trauma. Granted, there's nothing new about educators' concern in showing respect for diversity while making connections with individual kids. Yet new generational contexts in technology, family life, and social upbringing now require new frameworks for educating Alpha kids.

How do we—as families, teachers, and adult friends—teach Generation Alpha to live and to dream in this complex era? And what does it take to teach our children to fly?

The Generation Alpha megatrends explored in chapter 2 create conditions for our nation to realize what I call **transformative game changers** that can revolutionize the democratic traditions we will create for 2030. I think these three innovations can fundamentally and finally honor and celebrate our shared responsibility for the well-being of our nation's children.

- Game changer #1: Universal systems for supporting people, including paid family leave and greater visibility for unpaid work, must become the normative foundation from which both businesses and family life will thrive.

- Game changer #2: High-quality, tuition-free early childhood education should be available for all children everywhere if we are to reap the incontrovertible economic and social benefits that it produces for individuals, families, and communities.

- Game changer #3: Equity of opportunity for all Alpha children needs to become a unifying objective for family empowerment and mobilization. As key drivers of our children's futures, families must lead efforts to close achievement gaps, because in the diverse nation that we already are and will increasingly become, we can no longer prosper if large numbers of our children are left behind.

What makes these three game changers transformative? Taking steps to provide all people with more support, early childhood education, and opportunity is the key to the future because, if these game changers are realized, amazing things will happen:

1. We will fundamentally and comprehensively honor, focus attention on, and celebrate our shared responsibility for the well-being of our nation's children to a much greater degree than we do today.

2. We will shift our perspectives, recognizing that philosophies such as the "self-made man" have lost meaning or create dysfunction in the context of Generation Alpha's megatrend realities.

3. We will face—boldly! —the current and widespread dilemmas and crises we confront in raising and teaching Generation Alpha. Child care, for example, is in crisis because it shortchanges children, families, and teachers. Working families at all income levels have difficulty locating it, paying for it, and being assured that it is of the quality required to produce optimal outcomes for children, families, and society. Teachers in these settings share the brunt of this crisis through low compensation and poor working conditions. The COVID-19 pandemic shed light on these structural inequities.

4. We will make important and lasting changes in our existing national infrastructure in ways that are inspired by the Generation Alpha megatrends while also improving the quality of life for all generations.

5. We will acknowledge widespread variance within our population diversity and consciously decide to disrupt group disparities that do not serve us well given our changing demographics. (Read more about how we can do this in the final chapter.)

6. We will transform the latent (unexpressed) desires of families and early childhood educators into actionable demands on behalf of all Alpha children.

So, how do we as the adults in children's lives produce these transformations? While the Generation Alpha megatrends offer us the context to become transformative, transformative progress is not yet guaranteed for families who need support, for young children who need an education, and for our nation, which desperately needs equity of opportunity. One goal of this book is to encourage action among individuals, as well as communities of families and teachers, who share the mission of trying to make life better for our children and ourselves. Our transformative agency depends on our commitment to focus on both the here and now as well our ability to promote social change.

> **game changer**
>
> . . . an event, idea or procedure that effects a significant shift in the current manner of doing or thinking about something.
>
> —*Lexico*

The final chapter of this book offers three strategies to realize this commitment: mobilizing citizens, using an equity lens, and choosing to transform, not just conform to, social systems. These strategies are critical adaptations to the world that we are now entering, a world in which

- innovations in artificial intelligence change the nature of work and redefine the roles of individuals who do the work;

- variations in the size or racial composition of generations result in larger numbers of two groups, young people of color and the elderly; and

- strong evidence exists about the short- and long-term benefits of a developmentally appropriate early education for young children, family support, and equity of opportunity.

It is important to note that these game changers are NOT

- political party platforms. Game changers are strategies in the national interest for everyone.
- ideological positions. Game changers are responses to demographic and social realities.
- special interests. Game changers will benefit all of our children, while promoting national unity and strength.

Are these game changers achievable? Most certainly they are.

Indeed, if Generation Alpha represents inevitable new circumstances, and if we as adults are to establish game changers that support the Alphas' journeys, we must look more closely at our transformative capacity to create game changers. We must analyze and act to remediate inequalities that could jeopardize or threaten our nation's potential to create systems of equity among us.

Just as Generation Alpha represents a future *promise*, there are contemporary *disruptors* that, left undisturbed and unchecked, can limit or eradicate the opportunities that Generation Alpha represents. Allowed to persist, inequalities within our nation can increase social tensions that perpetuate Fixed Nation inclinations. Frontline proactive investments in support for people, early childhood education, and equity of opportunity will pave the way for our children's success. Change is not an option—it is a requirement if we are to realize a Fluid Nation with opportunities that transcend demography, preserve our representative democracy, and increase justice in our society.

Are these game changers achievable? Whatever the challenges in store, we must certainly try to achieve them.

In the next chapters we will highlight each of these three transformative innovations to better understand the problems being presented to Generation Alpha, to highlight how other countries are addressing these problems, and to propose solutions. What works in one country may fail in another. But there are important lessons from other nations that may inform our thinking and expand our aspirations.

TRANSFORMATIVE GAME CHANGER #1: UNIVERSAL SYSTEMS FOR SUPPORTING PEOPLE

Pain Points:

- Life expectancy decreased
- Elders aging alone lacking support
- Women's choice to be employed suppressed

Game Changers:

- Visibility and respect for unpaid labor
- Paid family leave
- Cash benefits/universal basic income

IV

TRANSFORMATIVE

Game Changer #1: Universal Systems for Supporting People

For more than two centuries, the American Dream has rested on several fundamental themes: meritocracy, self-reliance, independence, and personal responsibility. Widely celebrated in our culture is the notion of the individual, ostensibly from some impoverished or disadvantaged background, who achieves eminence through hard work and perseverance, without inheritance, family connections, or other privileges. Indeed, the "self-made man" (or woman) who "pulls himself up by his bootstraps" is a powerful paradigm of the American Dream. While these ideas have been critiqued extensively, they have nevertheless inspired countless millions to embrace the bold idea that everyone—indeed *anyone*!—regardless of race, class, or gender, can not only expect but also receive justice and fair play from society to match the extent of their personal effort.

But beneath the bravado is the reality that often accompanying hard work, determination, and perseverance are social structures and public policies that create the conditions for individual success—or failure. Ta-Nehisi Coates demonstrates the "compounding moral debts" of discriminatory practices that have made "bootstrapping" virtually impossible for many people of color, especially in terms of housing, education, and child welfare. [90] Even Michael Young, who popularized the term

> "The American dream, that has lured tens of millions of all nations to our shores in the past century has not been a dream of merely material plenty, though that has doubtlessly counted heavily. It has been much more than that. It has been a dream of being able to grow to fullest development as man and woman, unhampered by the barriers which had slowly been erected in the older civilizations, unrepressed by social orders which had developed for the benefit of classes rather than for the simple human being of any and every class."[91]
>
> —James Truslow Adams, promoter of the term American Dream in his 1931 book The Epic of America

meritocracy in his 1958 book *The Rise of the Meritocracy*, holds out little hope that meritocratic forms of selection will necessarily be equitable, let alone egalitarian, without improving the equality of opportunity across all of society.[92]

So how do we lead and motivate our children, providing them with essential foundations for both personal and generational success? Many of us are unsure what we can or should do.

Few families of Alpha kids will advise them to rely solely on either their own bootstraps or their family connections to reach their own American Dream. To support their parenting, mothers, more than fathers, have extensive support networks they count on for advice, turning to family members, friends, social media, and reference materials. But will parenting resources alone show us how to facilitate our children's American Dream?

Likewise, early childhood educators often are unsure of how to change the dynamics surrounding their professional practice—either to better serve children or to improve their own circumstances. With respect to Alpha children, educators are encouraged to reward effort to become smarter so that students will develop a growth mindset marked by resilience and a thirst for mastery. A growth mindset, therefore, would equip these Alpha kids with the intellectual flexibility and disposition to create their American Dreams in their own contexts. But will this type of guidance, absent equity of opportunity, help us lead our children toward their American Dream?

Success for the Alpha generation must include and extend far beyond parenting books and growth mindsets as childrearing and teaching strategies. Knowing the megatrends shaping our children, an essential ingredient to their success must be the creation of public policies that create more universal and equitable frameworks that reimagine the American Dream in the twenty-first century. These policy creations are game changers that go beyond calls for "self-reliance," "personal responsibility," and "family independence" to recognize the social and policy structures that underlie individual and group success.

> In an 1872 lecture, Frederick Douglass argued that there were "no such men as self-made men. That term implies an individual independence of the past and present which can never exist. . . . Our best and most valued acquisitions have been obtained either from our contemporaries or from those who have preceded us in the field of thought and discovery. We have all either begged, borrowed or stolen. We have reaped where others have sown, and that which others have strown, we have gathered."[93]

HOW OUR PEER NATIONS SUPPORT FAMILIES

How—and how well—do other countries support family functioning and well-being? Researchers from the University of Texas examined surveys of well-being from twenty-two nations and found that feeling happy as a parent is directly tied to the country where you live and how well public policies in that country support your family role. For example, parents in Norway, Sweden, Finland, Hungary, and Russia say they are even happier than their childless peers. Parents in the United States have the largest happiness shortfall compared to people who don't have children.[94]

> "What we found was astonishing. The negative effects of parenthood on happiness were *entirely* explained by the presence or absence of social policies allowing parents to better combine paid work with family obligations. And this was true for both mothers *and fathers*. Countries with better family policy "packages" had no happiness gap between parents and non-parents. . . . Furthermore, the . . . policies that helped parents the most were policies that also improved the happiness of everyone in that country, whether they had children or not."[95]
>
> *—Reflections by Jennifer Glass, sociology professor, University of Texas, on her twenty-two country survey of parental happiness.*

The World Economic Forum's Global Social Mobility Index ranks eighty-two countries on their success in supporting the upward mobility of its citizens from all social backgrounds. The most successful nations were the Nordic countries and some other parts of Europe. The top performers in order are Denmark, Norway, Finland, Sweden, and Iceland. The United States ranks twenty-seventh.[96]

Millennial families aware of international family support systems realize that the United States lags behind in offering these essential services. They realize there are consequences for the lack of support. But they know we can do better. Here are three realities that we face in the United States:

1. Economic mobility within and across generations— one of the key drivers of the American Dream and the self-made man philosophy—occurs to a much lesser extent than we imagine. In the United States we have historically been optimistic that regardless of our family background, working hard, being smart, and having talent will give us a reasonable chance for upward social and economic mobility within our own lifetimes and certainly in the lifetimes of our children. As a result, every generation can be better off than the one that preceded it. As Julia Issacs, Isabel Sawhill, and Ron Haskins point out in their extensive analysis, this dream is complex and challenged, particularly for African Americans.[99] A family's economic position strongly influences the economic status of children when they become adults. Raj Chetty and others using income to measure mobility found that absolute upward economic mobility has been declining since the 1940s. For children born in the 1940s, more than 90 percent earned more than their parents at the same age, but only about 50 percent of those born in 1980 have earned more than their parents at the same age.[100]

More, despite ideals to the contrary, the facts show that economic mobility in the United States is not exceptional relative to many other nations. Indeed, the United States was found to have the least mobility of thirteen nations in the Organisation for Economic Co-operation and Development (OECD).[101]

2. The United States remains the only member of the OECD that doesn't guarantee workers paid family leave. State analyses continue to show limited progress in this area. In 2018 the Bureau of Labor Statistics reported that only 17 percent of civilian workers could get paid time off to take care of a family member. The Family Medical Leave Act provision for unpaid leave is available to 59 percent of workers,

"Individuals born into poorer families have a better chance of owning a home, getting a good education and experiencing a better life than their parents if they are born in Canada than if they are born in the United States."[97]

—*Hanna Ziady, CNN*

"It's easier to be poor in Canada than in the U.S. I don't think Canadian kids are ahead of us for genetic reasons; Canada has made a wide range of social policy decisions differently. The kind of society that we live in really shapes what we see at kindergarten entry. And we can make policy decisions that change that."[98]

—*Douglas Downey, sociologist, The Ohio State University*

although many workers indicate that they cannot afford to take off under these provisions. About half of US women take less than two months of maternity leave, and nearly one in four women return to work within two weeks of giving birth.[102]

3. The child care challenge is a big part of the problem. Young families from all walks of life lament the Herculean challenge of finding affordable and high-quality child care while maintaining employment. Of the thirty-six nations that are members of the OECD, the United States is one of the five least-affordable nations for child care, as measured by percentage of family income. The United States also spends much less than other countries on helping families pay for child care. Although the OECD nations average 0.7 percent of gross domestic product on early childhood education and care, countries vary widely—Sweden spends 1.6 percent, Iceland spends 1.8 percent, and the United States spends just 0.3 percent.[104]

> "There's an incredible anxiety around parenting here that I just don't feel in other countries."[103]
>
> —*Christine Gross-Loh, author of* Parenting Without Borders

PAIN POINTS RELATED TO LIMITED FAMILY SUPPORT

As it turns out, "bootstrapping" puts quite a strain on family life and can be fairly stress inducing. Low levels of support for people have real consequences for our society:

Pain point #1: Lower life expectancy for both children and adults. One paper suggested that Americans would live nearly four years longer if the United States had a safety net as generous as those of European countries.[105] Estimates suggest that every year about six hundred infant deaths could be prevented if the United States had twelve weeks of paid family leave.[106]

Pain point #2: As they become adults, Generation Alpha is likely to experience worry about elders, particularly the growing number of elder orphans, those people (mostly women) who are aging alone with fewer traditional sources of support such as adult children, a spouse, relatives, or others to rely on for company and help during their senior years. Maria T. Carney reported that almost one fourth of elders aged sixty-five or more were aging alone without significant support.[107] In a 2015 report released by the US Department of Health and Human Services, about 29 percent of all older persons lived alone—36 percent of older women (and 46 percent of women aged seventy-five and over), and 20 percent of older men.[108] Worry about elders is likely to increase as Gen Alpha (with no or few siblings to help them) reaches adulthood, due to both the elders' extended life-span as well as the large number of elders likely to need some level of support.

Pain point #3: Reduced productivity within the workforce. Absenteeism and lost productivity due to child care crises cost employers about $3 billion a year.[109] Because subsidized child care has been documented to significantly impact women's employment in industrialized

SUPPRESSION OF WOMEN'S CHOICE TO BE EMPLOYED

The Department of Labor's former Chief Economist Heidi Shierholz estimated that if US women between twenty-five and fifty-four participated in the labor force at the same rate as they do in Canada or Germany, there would be more than five million more women in the US labor force, which could translate into more than $500 billion of additional economic activity per year. If the United States implemented family support policies about as generous as the average ones in other developed countries, women's labor force participation would rise nearly seven points.[110]

nations, child care is perhaps one of the largest barriers to gender equity in the workplace.

- The United States has declined as a leader in women's labor force participation. We ranked sixth out of twenty-two wealthy economies in 1990. By 2017 we ranked twentieth.[111] Explanations for stalled women's employment have focused on the cost of child care and school schedules.

- It helps the economy when women are employed. It's often economically beneficial for their families, too, especially since up to 40 percent of women are the sole or primary provider in households with children.[112] In families that can't find child care, the mother's likelihood of employment, but not the father's, was strongly impacted. Not surprisingly, those most affected are low-income women of color.

- In addition to the advantages for children when Washington, DC, initiated two years of universal full-day preschool, there was a 10 to 12 percent increase in maternal labor force participation. The two years of free early childhood education that the District of Columbia provides has allowed women to contribute to the gross

AMAZON MOMS

In March 2019, mothers working for Amazon protested that they were "tired of seeing colleagues quit because they can't find child care," noting that the "lack of affordable child care stopped talented women from progressing in their careers." They asked their employer to join other large companies, such as Apple, Microsoft, and Google, in offering emergency backup child care services. They succeeded for themselves but noted that "employers can't solve the nation's child care crisis alone, and a few days of back-up child care do not meet the needs of parents who must coordinate and pay for full-time year-round care."[113]

domestic product, improve the financial security of their households, and choose to be employed since their children were engaged
in preschool during the day.[114]

STRATEGIES TO ACHIEVE GAME CHANGER #1: UNIVERSAL SYSTEMS FOR SUPPORTING PEOPLE

We recommend three basic strategies to achieve game changer #1: giving
visibility and respect to unpaid household work, enacting universal paid
family leave, and exploring universal basic income supports.

**Strategy #1: Give visibility and respect to the unpaid work it takes
to manage everyday life within households.** Caring for Alpha children,
the elderly, and the ill is typically invisible physical and emotional labor
that falls primarily on women in most societies. Though difficult to define
and measure, this "cognitive labor," as Allison Daminger describes it,[115]
is an essential function that goes unrecognized by almost everyone except
the person doing it. Invisible labor, though time consuming and unpaid,
could equal about 13 percent of global GDP—and $2.1 trillion in the
United States alone—if given market value.[116]

Strategy #2: Enact universal paid family leave policies. Besides
recognizing the value of invisible unpaid work, paid leave offers important benefits to both employers and employees. Providing paid sick time
to employees reduces the spread of illness, increases productivity, and
improves public health. The danger of losing a job or missing a promotion
because of illness, pregnancy, or caregiving duties leaves too many family
members having to choose between their families and their jobs.

This is an area in which the United States lags significantly behind
other countries but around which there is growing enthusiasm for making
changes. Both political parties are taking notice of these challenges, and
public demand is emerging. As of 2020, at least eight states as well as the
District of Columbia have passed laws that require workers or their employees to make payroll contributions into state-paid leave funds. In 2019
President Donald Trump signed a bill that, for the first time, will provide
up to 12 weeks of paid leave for the federal government's 2.1 million

civilian employees following the birth, adoption, or fostering of a child, taking effect in late 2020.

Although differing on the specifics, in general Americans support paid family and medical leave.[117] We should begin to move forward by

- guaranteeing at least three months of paid family and medical leave yearly, with an assurance of job security upon return from leave; and

- using an equity lens to ensure that family leave policies are gender neutral, and encompass all types of families; and set minimum income eligibility levels so that lower-wage workers can afford to take paid family and medical leave without being unduly penalized.

Strategy #3: Explore the feasibility of offering cash benefits to families such as universal basic income (UBI) or child benefits. This is a game changer because it affects how we think about government assistance. Cash benefits also recognize the need to stem the tide of the dramatic increases in income inequality that the United States has been experiencing over the past four decades.

A UBI is a government guarantee that each citizen receives a minimum income or payment. As far back as 1967, Martin Luther King Jr. expressed confidence that a guaranteed income would help abolish poverty. King thought it cruel to ask bootless people to lift themselves up by their own bootstraps.

Various versions of this concept have been conducted or piloted by organizations and governments in Finland, Italy, Uganda, Cambodia, Kenya, Canada, India, and in several US locations. Providing a UBI assumes that anyone—particularly Alpha generation children—can benefit from stability and support. A UBI has potential to address the changing US economy and soften the impact of automation and globalization on many workers.

Whether cash transfer programs will be effective or not has yet to be firmly established empirically. What is established is that poverty harms child development. Our growing income inequality walks hand in hand with a gap in children's test scores. And, there are some indications that giving families income supplements could have positive effects on their children's educational outcomes, especially if the income supplements come during early childhood.

Game changers that offer greater support to people—such as family leave or universal basic income—emerge as responses to human needs. Many people will shudder at the high costs of making these changes, but doing nothing also exacts costs borne by individuals and by our society as a whole. Yes, this is a critical social issue and also an important economic challenge, as these strategies open up our nation's financial and intellectual capacity by closing gender gaps and adding value to our GDP. Whatever is done is unlikely to yield widespread immediate relief. But we must keep a vision of progress in mind, realizing that a more equitable tomorrow can be achieved only as a result of actions we take today.

TRANSFORMATIVE GAME CHANGER #2: UNIVERSAL HIGH-QUALITY, TUITION-FREE EARLY CHILDHOOD EDUCATION

Pain Points:

- Inaccessible

- Unaffordable

- Uneven quality

- Workforce inequities

Game Changers:

- Paid family leave

- Universal high-quality, tuition-free early childhood education

TRANSFORMATIVE

Game Changer #2: Universal High-Quality, Tuition-Free Early Childhood Education

Strategies such as universal basic income have yet to be fully proven in our society. Much about the effectiveness of that strategy is unknown. But as we consider the game changer of early childhood education, we face a different dilemma: We actually *know* more than we *do.* Indeed, we have more than six decades of research about and experience with early childhood education. Nevertheless, we have failed to build programs or systems that embrace the knowledge base, creating gaps between research, practice, and funding.

The result of these gaps, after being prolonged for decades, is a full-blown crisis for the Alpha children in the United States, an everyday dilemma occurring in plain sight that has catastrophic effects on children, families, early childhood educators, and employers. Volumes have been written about this situation in both the academic and popular press. Yet our nation seems paralyzed, unable to move forward or act on either the human needs or the scientific knowledge that is right in front of us. The volumes written on this topic make the case for a new paradigm, but the current paradigm stubbornly refuses to shift. This is particularly puzzling because we are a nation that prizes innovation and progress based on science and common sense.

Still, fundamental paradigm shifts often advance slowly. Thomas Kuhn's paradigm shift concept, developed for the natural sciences but often used in the social sciences, refers to profound change in the perception of situations. A paradigm shift is a significant change in theory or practice, a conceptual breakthrough that creates a new normal phase of operating. When there is a paradigm shift in early childhood education, for example, inexplicable results start piling up, eventually leading to what Kuhn describes as a "crisis."

Kuhn's crises are readily apparent in early childhood education right now. A reasonable response to the crisis would be to move from "fix-it" approaches, such as continual requests for additional funds for low-income child care vouchers, to creating systems that serve all children and families in entirely new and different ways. We have struggled with this crisis for many decades, but now in the twenty-first century, the evidence for change is irrefutable.

OUR CURRENT STATE

In the face of inaction, inexplicable results have piled high.

1. Families want and need early childhood education. Most of the more than 20 million children under five years of age spend a significant part of the day with an adult other than a parent or family member. Nonparental child care is now the norm.[118]

2. Alpha kids benefit from early childhood education, just as previous generations also benefitted. Past and present evidence demonstrates the value of early childhood education.

> "Nobody has ever before asked the nuclear family to live all by itself in a box the way we do. With no relatives, no support, we've put it in an impossible situation."[119]
>
> —Margaret Mead, cultural anthropologist

For example, children who attended 1940s-era child care centers established to support the war effort had better educational and economic outcomes throughout their lives, especially compared with children who were too young to participate. This held true especially for children from low-income families.[120] The evidence suggests that today's Alpha kids can reap similar benefits. Through a highly regarded synthesis of the impact of early childhood education programs, a panel of distinguished researchers determined that kindergarten preparation was better for children who attended public preschool programs, compared to children who did not. And children who are disadvantaged, low income, or dual-language learners often made the most gains.[121]

3. Early childhood education is a proven economic asset for our nation. Our entire society wins when we invest in our young—and these economic gains extend for generations, often more than paying for themselves. A plethora of studies have established as much as a 13 percent return on investment, based on calculations of improved life outcomes in education, health, social interactions, employment, and other areas both for mothers and for children when they become adults.[122] There is unmistakable majority consensus among policy analysts, scholars, and families that investments in children are essential to prosperity, both for the children personally and for our country as a whole.

4. Employers and our military reap rewards too. In an analysis of children over the course of thirty-five years, Nobel Prize–winning economist James Heckman concluded that high-quality early childhood programs strengthen today's workforce and prepare future generations to be more competitive.[123] As further evidence, as part of its military readiness strategy, the armed services of the United States operates what is widely considered to be one of the highest quality child care systems in our nation.

In the face of this strong evidence, why has financial support for early childhood education lagged so far behind? When it comes to our young children, we as a nation hesitate to take action. Yet if the early childhood education system isn't working for anyone, why has there been so little effective movement for transformative change? Why hasn't there been a policy paradigm shift?

ANALYZING THE GAP

At least three major inexplicable results have piled up: barriers of cultural mythologies; limited focus of children's policy; and a bevy of worries about the impact of child care, specifically as it relates to the roles of women and people of color.

Issue #1: Early childhood education must overcome the barrier of cultural mythologies. Quite frankly, our nation is caught up in the myth of self-sufficiency and family self-reliance. Unless you have some type of deficiency—like poverty, abuse, or an extraordinary need that makes you stand out—our ethos holds that you and your family should take care of yourselves. After all, isn't this the core instinct that enabled the expansion of our nation into the frontier and motivated brave Midwestern home-steaders to create new communities? This myth runs deep, wrapped up with our notions of freedom and independence and the "American way."

Spoiler alert! The truth of modern life is that while each of us abso-lutely should do for ourselves what we can do, none of us is a modern homesteader, and we are never likely to be self-sufficient in twenty-first century America. We all rely on community and public resources to a large extent in our daily lives. The water that supplied your daily shower and other key utilities are all part of shared resources that make modern life possible. The reality is that we're better off, more prosperous, and have higher standards of living with more opportunities for people to be creative because of our network of relationships, social capital, and public services.

Issue #2: The direct beneficiaries of early childhood education— the Alpha children themselves—can't vote for their own needs, and the political influence of early childhood education advocates is relatively weak. Exhausted parents, personally scrambling to pay what amounts to about 60 percent of what the program costs, have little time or mental en-ergy to try to change the complex child care frameworks in our nation.[124] Rather, their efforts are focused on surviving the years before the start of their children's free public education. While one might assume that the child care crisis would make it easy for parents to mobilize for public action, their frustration with the system leaves them more likely to focus on their immediate problems rather than engaging in activism, actually making it harder to address the broader public policy issues. Similarly, al-though celebrating many victories over the years, child advocates confront significant asymmetrical conflicts, including imbalances of power and access to resources, that impede or block progress.

Issue #3: Perhaps most importantly, throughout American history we have had conflicting feelings about child care, feelings that were often tied to our views about race, poverty, and the role of women. Traditionally, many people in the United States have held to the idea that women do not belong in the workforce, except in wartime or if they were poor or Black. To give just one example, in the early 1900s White women, relative to impoverished Black women, were the disproportionate beneficiaries of "Mother's Pensions" that supported single mothers to stay home with their children. Even today, most Americans continue to believe that being raised by two working parents is an imperfect scenario for children.[125] In stark contrast, there's been a different ideal for poor families, who since 1996 have been required to work when receiving public assistance and the child care subsidies they may need.

The Boomer generation fretfully discussed these questions: Will "day care" hurt kids? Is it safe? Does it reflect our values? The debate was still on in 1971 when President Richard Nixon vetoed the Comprehensive Child Development Act, which had been approved by Congress to create universal child care. He reflected the views of many Americans who resisted feminist demands and the idea of women in the workforce when he asserted that the bill (and child care in general) had "family-weakening implications," was "a long leap into the dark," and would "commit the vast moral authority of the National Government to the side of communal approaches to child rearing over against the family-centered approach," tying child care to broad-based fears of communism that were prevalent at that time.[126]

These views persist decades later, according to research showing that Americans cling to traditional views of daily life. These views, of course, vary across generations: the older you are, the more likely you are to say young children are better off with an at-home parent. About 64 percent of those over sixty-five express that view, compared with about 61 percent of those ages fifty to sixty-four, 57 percent of those age thirty to forty-nine, and 54 percent of those younger than thirty. This 2016 Pew Research Center survey also found that 59 percent of Americans say the

"One of my male partners told me flat-out that I and our other female partners who have kids should really be spending more time at home and should send new patients to him or the other male partners. My jaw just dropped. When I expressed disbelief, he said something like, 'What? If you're not interested in spending time with your kids, that makes you a bad mother.' I don't think he had any idea at all what's wrong with saying that. Especially since we're in the field of women's medicine, you'd think there'd be a sense of irony at treatment like this. I was pressured to work during a four-week maternity leave!"[128]

—A gynecologist sharing her experiences as a mother in the workforce, 2018

ideal situation for a young child in a two-parent household is for one parent to stay at home.[127]

Nevertheless, women's participation in the workforce continues to increase, with an accordant rise in early childhood education. The Boomer generation debated the merits of preschool, but for most Generation Alpha kids, the matter of merit is settled, and parents are voting with their enrollments, a phenomenon that represents a clear and absolute "inexplicable result" because it is occurring despite weaknesses in our nation's child care policies. Even Millennial staff who do not have children nevertheless indicate that child care considerations were a big part of their decision to accept a job.[129]

Stubbornly, public policy lags behind parental demand for early childhood education. The lack of public support for child care creates widespread inequity for children, limits enrollment of children from all backgrounds, ensures the persistence of child care deserts, puts financial strain on families, and puts pressure on the bottom line for child care employers while simultaneously undervaluing and impoverishing the staff who work with young children.

HOW OUR PEER NATIONS DO IT BETTER

While the United States wavers on early childhood education, other nations are moving forward more decisively. Sharon Lynn Kagan and a team of her colleagues recently examined how six countries provide early childhood education, concluding that both per-child spending and total pre-primary enrollment in the United States lag far behind comparable nations. All of the countries studied for Kagan's report—*The Early Advantage 2—Building Systems That Work for Young Children: International Insights from Innovative Early Childhood Systems*—included low-income populations and a range of cultures (Hong Kong, Australia, the United Kingdom, Finland, Korea, and Singapore). Yet none of them make a certain income level a requirement for services. Services in these countries tend to include comprehensive health benefits, parenting supports, and near-universal guarantees for children aged three and four with options for the care of babies and toddlers. In contrast, the United States offers no consistent programs or plans.[130]

Focusing primarily on countries in the European Union, the American Institutes for Research identified five integrated and reinforcing themes that seem to contribute to the high levels of participation in early childhood education: legal entitlement to services; strong and stable financial support for the system; connecting children to the system early; community connections between systems and the families they serve; and targeted support for integrating immigrants and addressing inequality in society.[131]

Most OECD countries now offer universal or near-universal access to at least one year of early childhood education. Despite enrollment growth in the United States, we continue to lag far behind other OECD nations in the enrollment of young children in early childhood education programs, ranking twenty-ninth out of thirty-four nations.[132] Our enrollment rates, virtually unchanged since 2005, are 39 percent for children aged three and 68 percent for children aged four. On the other hand, enrollment rose across OECD member countries from 54 percent in 2004 to 71 percent in 2014 for three-year-olds and from 73 percent to 85 percent for four-year-olds.[133] While this international comparison data is less current, it indicates a pattern of the United States' failure to create a paradigm shift in early childhood education.

PAIN POINTS RELATED TO EARLY CHILDHOOD EDUCATION

Whereas other countries have prioritized the development of early childhood education systems, our nation faces unique endemic pain points that reflect what we actually do in contrast to what we actually know. Here, we synthesize these pain points as the interrelationships of

- *access* to early childhood education;
- the *quality* of early childhood education; and
- the gestalt of financing and market forces that influence both *affordability* for parents and workforce *compensation*.

Permeating each of these pain points are issues of equity, a core concern for the Alpha generation. The relationship between race and income and a person's access to high-quality early childhood education is a central barrier to equity for Alpha children. Achieving equity requires us to integrate access, price, and quality across everything we do for young children. To truly use tuition-free early childhood education as a game changer for this generation, we must see these four components—access, quality, financing, and equity—not as dichotomous but as overlapping and interdependent concepts.

Here are the four pain points: accessibility, affordability, quality, and workforce issues—each of which has equity concerns.

PAIN POINT #1: PROGRAMS ARE INACCESSIBLE

Finding child care is a daunting task for almost everyone . . . Child care options are scarce and inconvenient for almost everyone; at least 62 percent of parents across income groups face difficulty in finding it.[134] More than 79 percent of both Democrats and Republicans state repeatedly that child care should become a high national priority.[135]

. . . especially if you're looking for infant and toddler care.
Estimates suggest that existing programs have spots for only 10 percent of all children under one. For all children under three, the capacity is about 25 percent. One study of eight states found that 65 percent of child care centers do not serve children age one or younger and that 44 percent do not serve children under age three at all.[136]

The search is even worse for Black, Latinx, or poor families . . .
While many parents—39 percent—report that they have a hard time finding satisfactory options for their kids, Black families (56 percent) and poor families (52 percent) report even greater difficulty.[137] Another study suggests that Hispanic families look for but cannot find appropriate, accessible care for their children.[138]

. . . or if you are the half of America that lives in a child care desert. Millions of Alpha children under the age of five live in child care deserts, places where there isn't enough licensed child care for families that need it. Overall, child care deserts are three times more likely to be populated by Hispanics.[139] Also heavily affected are families living in rural areas, immigrant families, Native American or Alaska Native families, and families with nontraditional or shifting work hours.

As a result, half of children at all income levels experience multiple, and often unstable, child care arrangements. The Center for American Progress reported that nearly one-quarter of children use three or more arrangements.[140] And lower-income families rely more heavily on care by family, friends, and neighbors than on child care centers or preschools.

PAIN POINT #2: PROGRAMS ARE UNAFFORDABLE

Just as child care inaccessibility can lead families to select multiple child care arrangements, or to rely on their familial networks, the high cost of child care has a similar effect.

If you do find an early childhood education program, the price will probably strain your family budget. The US Department of Health and Human Services defines affordable child care as no more than 10 percent of a family's income. But typical families find that it takes about one-fifth of their household income to pay for a child care center spot.

For parents making a minimum wage, child care costs could be about two-thirds of their earnings. Child care is a significant budget item for a family—at about $9,589, child care costs are greater than in-state college tuition ($9,410). Child care is also the second-largest line item in the family budget, only exceeded by the mortgage or rent.[141]

How are families paying for these services? Lindsay Oncken of New America describes the costs as follows:

- Most of the payment comes out of the family pocketbook. Overall costs are distributed as follows: 60 percent from families; 39 percent from governments; and one percent from business and philanthropy.

- Working parents looking to offset child care costs can use the Child and Dependent Care Tax Credit (CDCTC), which as of 2020 was capped at $3,000.

- Although this tax credit has several limitations, 61 percent of businesses offer employees Dependent Care Assistance Plans to help them pay for care with up to $5,000 pretax dollars a year, according to the 2014 National Study of the Employer.[142]

About one in six eligible children from low-income, working families has access to child care subsidies and vouchers, although these subsidy systems are riddled with obstacles such as long waiting lists, low reimbursement rates, limited eligibility, and user dissatisfaction.[143] When child care centers, frustrated by low reimbursement rates or administrative requirements, opt out of subsidy systems, parents once again may find it necessary to choose unregulated family, friend, or neighbor care. This leaves children vulnerable to situations in which the quality of care they receive is unknown.

PAIN POINT #3: PROGRAMS ARE OF UNEVEN QUALITY

No matter how much you pay, your child's program may not meet expert standards for quality. Only a very small number of early childhood education programs, about 11 percent, have earned accreditation from one of the two main organizations that oversees it.[144] Over a long period of time, experts have defined what good early childhood education programs look like by measurable quality benchmarks, such as low teacher-child ratios of no more than 1:10; emphasis on family engagement; the quality of staff interactions and relationships with children; and the staff's level of professional certification, development, and compensation. According to the well-respected National Institute for Early Education Research, these essential benchmarks reflect the importance of more direct supports for the actual experiences that children have, primarily through interactions with teachers and peers.[145] And the experts report that most early childhood education in the United States is not meeting the quality standards. Child development researchers report that most child care in the United States is mediocre to poor, with approximately 9 to 10 percent considered very high quality.[146]

Nevertheless, the overwhelming majority of parents who use child care are happy with it, and 88 percent of parents say their child care is very good or excellent.[147]

So, why is there a disconnect between families and experts? Objectively, parents have many considerations when choosing programs for their children, including a location they prefer, staff they like, and a price they can bear. Parents clearly care about quality, but many parents don't know which quality indicators to look for. Also, it is difficult for parents who must work to admit that the place where they leave their child is somehow not up to expert standards, especially if they personally like the staff.

PAIN POINT #4: DISRESPECTED, UNDERCOMPENSATED, AND ILL-EQUIPPED STAFF

While the individual teacher with whom your child interacts may be personally dedicated and competent, that educator is likely to be undervalued and poorly paid. The staff's role is particularly salient in almost every indicator of program quality. Whether the measure of quality is the ratio of children to teachers, group size, or relationships, it is the early childhood educator who makes a substantial contribution to your child's experience. These educators are the active force that strengthens the social, emotional, and cognitive development of the millions of children who are in early childhood programs every day. But because many parents pay such a significant part of their family earnings for these services, many may be surprised to learn that the people to whom they entrust their children each day are often impoverished. Why? Simply stated: early childhood educators are often caught in a cycle in which insufficient program resources and high labor requirements almost inevitably result in reduced capacity to deliver the best practices of the profession. This reduced capacity then yields unsatisfactory consequences for children, families, educators, programs, and society. Then the cycle begins again because families can't pay more.

The cycle begins with insufficient resources to pay for the cost of quality. Child care market failure is legendary because so much of the early childhood education infrastructure is really a loosely organized network of tuition-driven small businesses, nonprofits, and family child care homes with 1 percent profit margins.[148] The relatively small contributions of government, philanthropy, and business are insufficient to ensure the delivery of high-quality services.

We face intensive labor requirements. Early childhood education is a people-intensive endeavor, and program safety and other quality requirements reflect the higher levels of supervision that young children require relative to older children. Personnel costs consume about 60 to 80 percent of program cost. The additional 20 percent to 40 percent covers rent, administration, and classroom expenses.[149] Consequently, payroll and related expenses become a prime target as owners and operators struggle to keep operational costs low in the face of insufficient resources. While state regulations allow one teacher for anywhere from eighteen to thirty elementary school children, early childhood professional standards are one teacher for every three or four infants, one teacher for every three to six toddlers, and one teacher for every six to ten preschoolers.[150]

The sum of intensive labor requirements plus low revenue due to market failure adds up to inadequate compensation. In the face of severe market failure, early childhood educators have earned very low wages for a long time. Data show, for example, that in 2016 early childhood educators earned among the lowest wages of any profession—on average $9.77 an hour for child care staff, $12.44 for self-employed home care staff, and $13.74 for preschool staff.[151] And the compensation of early childhood educators of color fares even worse than their White peers. Consequently, many staff qualify for public support in the form of food stamps, Medicaid, or even child care subsidies since they cannot afford to pay the cost of a program for their own children.

The age of the child and the setting in which one works appears to influence salaries more significantly than the educators' competencies or roles. For example, infant and toddler teachers earn about 70 percent of the salaries of three- and four-year-old teachers.[152] The national median annual wage for preschool teachers is 55 percent of the wages earned by kindergarten teachers and 52 percent of elementary school teachers' wages.[153] The Early Childhood Workforce Index characterizes the wage structure as irrationally linked to program funding pressures rather than meaningful indicators of the educators' skill or preparation.[154] Indeed, in most countries, not just the United States, despite needing a bachelor's degree, early childhood teachers earn less than their professional peers with a similar educational background.

The result is unsatisfactory consequences for children, families, educators, programs, and society. These consequences include job shortages, high staff turnover, the need to hire staff with limited training, and a lack of respect for the profession. Children subjected to less qualified or changing staff may be unable to develop the types of relationships important for their learning. As a result, programs are unable to meet quality benchmarks and suffer setbacks as they try to professionalize the field, especially when methods such as increasing educator credentials fail to improve wages. The cycle begins again because of market failure and families' inability to pay the full cost of high-quality programs.

STRATEGIES TO ACHIEVE GAME CHANGER #2: UNIVERSAL HIGH-QUALITY, TUITION-FREE EARLY CHILDHOOD EDUCATION

Given the realities summarized in the following table, two basic strategies could achieve game changer #2: providing paid family leave and instituting voluntary tuition-free early childhood education for all children in

GAME CHANGER: UNIVERSAL HIGH-QUALITY, TUITION-FREE EARLY CHILDHOOD EDUCATION

THE CURRENT STATE *WHAT WE KNOW*	THE CRISIS OF INEXPLICABLE RESULTS *THE GAP BETWEEN WHAT WE KNOW AND WHAT WE DO*	
Families want and need early childhood education.	We embrace national mythologies and ideal beliefs about family life despite visible realities and needs.	
Children and families benefit from early childhood education if it is high quality.	Ignoring decades of data, we tolerate inconsistent quality, a patchwork of loosely connected services, and low levels of adherence to quality benchmarks.	
Early childhood education is an economic asset to our nation.	We tolerate inequities for the very groups who could add significant economic value to our nation: women and mothers; children of color; and dual-language learners.	

	PAIN POINTS *WHAT WE DO*	BEYOND CRISES AND PAIN: GAME CHANGERS *COURAGE, VISION, AND STRATEGIES*
	We resist universal accessibility to early childhood education.	Next step: Create a vision for children based on our knowledge base and data.
	Our failure to design and finance systems for early childhood education make affordability a challenge for providers and families.	Next step: Design and implement comprehensive birth-to-five programs and finance policies that support strategies such as family leave, staff professionalization, and tuition-free early childhood education.
	We perpetuate inequities and provide insufficient quality programming even as our peer nations move forward and document the gains achieved.	Next step: Engage in public conversation and commit to transition strategies from our current patchwork of programs to a coherent integrated system of services.

any early childhood education setting (school, family child care, center, and so forth).

Strategy #1: Paid family leave is repeated as a game changer here, because families deserve the choice to provide at-home care for their own children.

Strategy #2: Voluntary tuition-free early childhood education for all children must become universally available and supported by government, employers, and communities. A third grader or a high school student is entitled to free public education in every state. The same should be true for all of our nation's children.

The latter idea will be a difficult one for some people to accept. Yet the option to choose early childhood education is essential for the Alpha generation. And history provides us with hope for change. Universal public education and the education of Blacks were once considered controversial, and now they are the norm. In turn, I believe attitudes toward universal, publicly supported early childhood education will also change, and our nation will come to recognize its value.

Clearly, tuition-free early childhood education should also be available for all of our nation's children. Here's a four-part roadmap:

- A series of public conversations about Alpha kids that help us to examine the philosophies and values underlying the gap between historic ideals and contemporary realities of gender roles and family life. Questions we might consider include the following: How might we unlink public support for early childhood education from eligibility requirements focused on poverty or special needs? By whom and by what quality standards do we want to raise Generation Alpha?

- State and national commissions focused on transition strategies from the current piecemeal approaches toward a coherent, long-overdue infrastructure investment in high-quality early childhood education. Just as our nation has put value on infrastructure investments in roads, bridges, and public buildings, we must allocate public resources toward improving access, quality, and affordability for Generation Alpha. And this infrastructure must be available to all, putting an end to child care deserts.

- School schedules that are better aligned with work schedules. Our basic design for school schedules hasn't changed much since the 1950s, a time when the archetypical White fathers worked while mothers were home to receive children from school in the mid-afternoon.

- A focus on improving the working conditions and economic viability of the early childhood education profession. For the benefit of children and families, the field will be able to attract and retain more highly qualified and experienced teachers and staff if salaries rise to become commensurate with their qualifications. High rates of turnover contribute to worsening teacher shortages, lower program quality, and discontinuity of care for children at this critical stage of their lives.

Efforts to achieve universal early childhood education will require enormous courage from the adults in the lives of Alpha children. Courage is required simply because so much is known about this topic, yet we as a society have tolerated the gaps for a very long time between what we know and what we actually do. Naming and facing the cultural mythologies, policy lapses, and worries about early childhood education can be a profound act of love for Generation Alpha—love that gives us the power to act.

> "Courage, the original definition of courage, when it first came into the English language—it's from the Latin word *cor*, meaning 'heart'—and the original definition was to tell the story of who you are with your whole heart."[155]
>
> —Brené Brown, professor, social worker, and New York Times best-selling author

It takes a lot of courage to let go of the old and to embrace the new and not-yet-secure future.

Remember, as educator activist Ericka Huggins tells us, that "love is an expression of power. We can use it to transform the world."[156] We will close the gap between what we know and what we do when we realize, in the words of Martin Luther King Jr., that "power without love is reckless and abusive . . . and love without power is sentimental and anemic."[157]

TRANSFORMATIVE GAME CHANGER #3: OPPORTUNITY EQUITY

Pain Points:

- Not investing early enough in the lives of young children

- High infant mortality rates

- Persistent poverty

- Large opportunity gaps

Game Changers:

- Empowering and mobilizing families for child development and social change

TRANSFORMATIVE

Game Changer #3: Opportunity Equity

Families need child care while the adults work or go to school. While families may have limited awareness of expert standards of care, they invest in early childhood education despite limited public support because they trust it as a tool to advance their children's social, physical, and intellectual capacities. Families in the United States have gotten the message: the child's environment matters—a lot! And families and teachers play a strong role in creating the environments that shape and predict child outcomes.

A highly valued child outcome in the United States is having a "smart" Alpha child, according to research by Sara Harkness and Charles M. Super. These researchers found that parents in the United States described their children in ways that highlighted their cognitive development and intelligence; nearly 25 percent of all the descriptors highlighted being "smart," "gifted," or "advanced." In other countries the descriptors tended to focus on social and emotional attributes such as being easy to parent and happy.[158] It is not uncommon for hyper-competitive and often economically advantaged parents to seem obsessed with perfecting their young children, expressing disappointment if their child becomes an "average" student. Parents in the United States offer enrichment experiences to their Alpha children, Harkness suggests, partly out of the need to push the children to reach their potential and partly out of the fear that their child will be left behind in an increasingly competitive and uncertain world.[159]

This conversation about opportunity equity poses questions about whether any child should be left behind. And, more importantly, what could we do now to get the best payoff for the entire *generation* of Alpha children? How might the status quo be disrupted so that the fortunes of Alpha children—and of our nation—are no longer cast along the lines of their racial and ethnic background? Any potential game changers for our nation must acknowledge and engage in this conversation about how we can help all Alpha children reach their full potential.

TWO PRESIDENTS SPEAK ABOUT EQUITY

"We . . . wish to allow the humblest man an equal chance to get rich with everybody else. When one starts poor, as most do in the race of life, free society is such that he knows he can better his condition; he knows that there is no fixed condition of labor for his whole life."[160]

—*President Abraham Lincoln*

"We are true to our creed when a little girl born into the bleakest poverty knows that she has the same chance to succeed as anybody else."[161]

—*President Barack Obama*

OPPORTUNITIES TO THRIVE IN OTHER NATIONS

Three basic cornerstones of opportunity equity for young children are the chance to be born healthy, to experience economic security, and to be welcomed into a society that has a foundation of educational supports to nurture and educate them. Nations, and indeed states within the United States, vary in their capacity to provide these three cornerstones for Alpha children.

Opportunity #1: To survive. Equity of opportunity begins with the basic chance to live and to grow up. The good news is that infant mortality rates around the world have been declining significantly. The concern is that infant mortality in the United States ranks poorly internationally, varies widely from state to state, and reflects enduring racial disparities. As an example, despite spending twenty times more per capita than Serbia, the infant mortality rate of the United States is comparable to Serbia's at 5.8 deaths per 1,000 live births. Out of 225 nations, the United States ranks fifty-fifth.[162]

Opportunity #2: To experience economic security. Poverty increases the likelihood of impaired brain development and poor academic, social, economic, and health outcomes, particularly if it is extended over time, begins at a young age, and remains persistent. It is therefore stunning to note that twenty percent of children in forty-one of the world's richest countries live in poverty, though this poverty is unevenly distributed among nations. Continuing a pattern shown in infant mortality data, international comparisons of poverty find the United States at the bottom of the list, ranking thirty-fifth of the forty-one countries surveyed. Relative poverty—defined by UNICEF as a household with income less than half the national median—is a reality for 30 percent of children in the United States.[163]

> "Among rich countries, the US is exceptional. We are exceptional in our tolerance of poverty."[164]
>
> —Sheldon Danziger, director of the National Poverty Center, University of Michigan

Opportunity #3: To achieve. International comparisons also reveal that students in nearly a dozen countries are improving academically two to three times faster than in the United States. These gains represent about two years of learning according to a 2020 report conducted by Harvard University's Program on Education Policy and Governance.[165] Sharon Lynn Kagan's analysis explained that all of the countries she studied offered far more services than the United States. Many other countries developed policies

GREATER INVESTMENTS YIELD LESS POVERTY

The opportunity for any Alpha child to experience economic security clearly results from a nation's choices. Research by Valerie Wilson and Jessica Schieder of the Economic Policy Institute found that child poverty is reduced when nations invest more money in social programs. For example, Denmark and Finland have child poverty rates below 4 percent and spend close to one-fifth of their GDP on social expenditures. In contrast, the United States has a 20 percent child poverty rate and spends 12 percent of GDP on social expenditures. Once again, the United States ranks at the bottom of international comparisons because we invest the third-lowest portion of GDP on social programs, surpassing only Slovenia and Slovakia.[166] A 2019 National Academy of Sciences consensus report found that the United States could reduce childhood poverty in half within ten years with specific and increased investments of $90 billion per year.[167]

more systemically so that the resulting systems and plans, like a national curriculum, were used to drive accountability, funding, and governance efforts.[168]

PAIN POINTS

Synthesizing all that we know about inequity, the Annie E. Casey foundation developed its Race for Results Index to measure how well-being and opportunity are distributed among children of different racial and ethnic backgrounds. The index shows that all children in the United States need support and no racial group is meeting all of the milestones. However, clear group differences were revealed. From a possible 1,000 points, index scores were in the 700s for Asian and Pacific Islander and White students (783 and 713 respectively), but fell much lower for Latino (429), American Indian (413), and African American students (369).[169]

The results of this index, along with international comparisons, give insight to four primary pain points: our failure to invest in children at their earliest stages of development in the first one thousand days of life; disproportionate rates of infant mortality; our tolerance for high rates of poverty among Alpha children; and decades of achievement gaps between groups of children. What all of these pain points share in common is that they are both persistent and preventable. Moreover, not one of them is randomly distributed. Each pain point exhibits statistically significant patterns of disproportionate impact by race and class.

Pain point #1: We don't invest early enough in the lives of our children. Recall that the Annie E. Casey index found that every group of children had room for growth on the milestones. This suggests a need for greater investment in *all* Alpha children. And in order to reap investments for Alpha children, we must better support teachers and families—the adults in their lives—with a more significant societal response.

For each individual child, parents and early educators have key responsibilities in building the relationships that every child requires in order to thrive. Many communities and advocates are now promoting the first one thousand days of life as a critical period in child development. Research in neuroscience and child development demonstrate that the nutrition, environment, and human interactions that children have at this time of life set tracks for the rest of a person's life.

But social and community investments matter too. We observe that annual per-child national spending levels in 2015 were about $16,600 for ages six to eighteen, $10,220 for three- to five-year-olds, and $8,820 for zero- to two-year-olds.[170] As a nation we invest the least when human development is at its fastest rate of growth. No wonder, then, that opportunity inequities begin early—well before kindergarten—when the country invests the least amount of its resources in children.

Pain point #2: One consequence of our low levels of investment is that infant mortality rates are too high. While infant mortality rates have generally trended downward since 1995, racial and ethnic disparities have persisted over time. Infant mortality rates are highest for infants of Black women.

Per one thousand births, the mortality rates in 2017 were as follows:

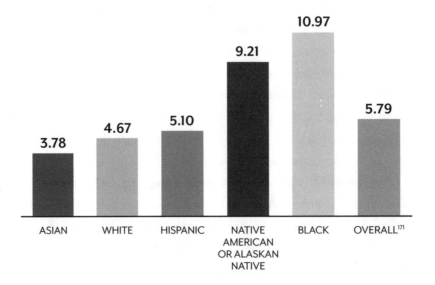

A HISPANIC PARADOX?

Ponder this: Why might it appear that Hispanics have infant mortality rates—and indeed, other health outcomes—more similar to Whites, even though their income and education is more similar to Blacks? This question forms "The Hispanic paradox." Some contend that health outcomes for Hispanics could be attributed to the strong family structure among Latinx. Others worry that this paradox exists only because Hispanic deaths are underestimated or counted inaccurately.

Pain point #3: From babyhood through childhood, we tolerate persistent poverty. The United States bears high rates of poverty, a factor that has ongoing negative impacts on child growth and development. These inequities fall disproportionately on children under five who are

Black, Native American, or Hispanic and who live in single-parent households or rural areas.

The good news is that poverty appears to be declining for *all* of our children, from 27 percent in 1960 to 18 percent in 2017.[172] While poverty rates for Black and Hispanic children have declined in the last forty years, Black and Hispanic children nonetheless represent almost two-thirds of children in poverty. Economists Valerie Wilson and Jessica Schieder explain this racial difference by observing that as people of color become a greater proportion of the nation's population, racial inequalities are magnified.[173] This fact emphasizes the critical importance of shifting our national funding priorities as we raise and educate Alpha children.

Pain point #4: The results of the status quo are, not surprisingly, persistently large academic gaps between racial groups—and diminished performance by all children. It is widely recognized that a child's reading skills by the end of third grade are a key indicator of future academic success. Yet in 2019, 65 percent of *all* fourth graders were reading below the proficient level, according to the National Assessment of Educational Progress.[174] The proportion of fourth graders reading below the proficient level for various population groups was as follows:

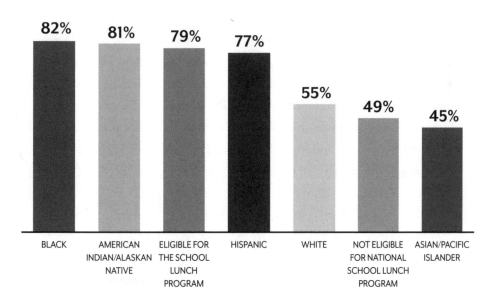

BLACK	AMERICAN INDIAN/ALASKAN NATIVE	ELIGIBLE FOR THE SCHOOL LUNCH PROGRAM	HISPANIC	WHITE	NOT ELIGIBLE FOR NATIONAL SCHOOL LUNCH PROGRAM	ASIAN/PACIFIC ISLANDER
82%	81%	79%	77%	55%	49%	45%

While some groups of children are obviously performing much worse than others, we cannot be satisfied when **no** group is performing very well.

Academic performance gaps emerge before children enter kindergarten and then tend to widen over time. Achievement gaps between Blacks, Whites, and Hispanics have become much smaller (in 2012, there had been perhaps a 40 percent decrease since the 1970s), although the disparities are still wide.[175] On average, the achievement gap can be roughly explained as the difference in performance between the average fourth grader and the average eighth grader.[176]

A HISTORY OF INEQUITY

We've worried about the achievement of all of our children—as well as inequities between them—for a long time. Yet our historic efforts to address gaps have fallen short. With clarity and insight, in 1954 the Supreme Court ruled in *Brown v. Board of Education of Topeka* that racial segregation in public schools was unconstitutional. Since the mid-twentieth century there have been several national-level analyses of the causes, effects, and cures of achievement gaps. While we can celebrate clear progress in the past six decades, there are unmistakable legacies embedded in our educational systems that, in essence, define opportunity inequity.

In the 1960s, the Kerner Commission investigation, intended to look into the causes of civil disorders, produced a strong and unanticipated finding: White racism fueled inequities of opportunity that led to pent-up frustration in communities of color. The Kerner Commission report stated bluntly: "Our nation is moving toward two societies, one black, one white—separate and unequal. . . . Discrimination and segregation have long permeated much of American life; they now threaten the future of every American."[177] No doubt, there has been progress since Kerner. But the ongoing relevance of the commission's essential conclusion was confirmed and reinforced in reports that marked its thirtieth, fortieth, and fiftieth anniversaries.

The James S. Coleman *Equality of Educational Opportunity* report of 1966 gave our nation the first comprehensive broad-scale data about the achievement discrepancies. Surveying about six hundred thousand children, sixty thousand teachers, and roughly four thousand schools, Coleman's work represented a substantive shift from research measuring educational inputs (such as funding, facilities, teacher or curricular quality, or extracurricular offerings) to research assessing educational outputs, outcomes, and effectiveness (measured largely in terms of student test scores). Coleman's findings—and the decades of analysis that have followed it—highlighted the role of families as well as schools in achievement outcomes.[178] In the heat of the civil rights movement, it also pointed to the deleterious effects of school segregation for Black and White students alike, as well as the importance of students' mindsets and motivation as contributors to their learning.

In 2002 the No Child Left Behind Act (NCLB) engendered a great deal of controversy through its focus on testing, teacher qualifications, and school choice. Nevertheless, one analysis found that, for African American, Hispanic, and low-income groups, achievement gaps typically narrowed in reading and math but nevertheless were 20 percentage points or more, a challenging gap to close. Another analysis noted NCLB's negative effects on the very populations that the law intended to help, including inappropriate testing of dual-language learners as well as pressure to exclude children of color from testing in ways that resulted in them dropping out of school or being classified in special education situations that were exempt from testing.[179]

In 2015 Congress replaced the increasingly unpopular NCLB with Every Student Succeeds Act (ESSA), which took full effect in the 2017–2018 school year. With its focus on greater local control over school decision-making, ESSA is most noteworthy for its explicit recognition of early learning in closing opportunity gaps, including the first-ever dedicated funding stream for early childhood education with the new Preschool Development Grant Birth through Five program. As of January 2019, forty-six states and territories were awarded funding through PDG B-5.[180] It is too early to know the impact of ESSA on children or on group achievement gaps.

LASTING LEGACIES

Five lasting legacies of opportunity inequity are relentless segregation; adverse, punitive learning environments; unequal teaching and learning resources; diminished opportunities to be recognized as excelling; and the new digital divide.

Relentless segregation. Despite Supreme Court rulings, Kerner's warnings, and decades of various interventions, racial isolation in programs still starts very young. A government report in 2016 found that, despite progress from the late 1960s through the 1980s, the percentage of schools that are racially and economically segregated had risen since 2001.[181] On average, Asian American preschool students are the only well-integrated group. White preschool students attend majority-White schools in almost every state. Black preschoolers typically

Ponder this: A question in the Coleman report asks students to select an image that looks most like their classmates.[182] How would Alpha children answer this question today?

attend minority-White schools (fewer than 25 percent White) in about half of all states, and only two states see Black preschoolers attending majority-Hispanic schools (California and New Mexico.) In no states does the average Hispanic preschooler attend majority-Black schools.[183]

Adverse, punitive learning environments. The academic achievement of children of color is no doubt diminished by the adverse and punitive academic culture that the children experience, even in preschool settings. Described as "violent," "dangerous," "hostile," and "aggressive,"[184] by the time they are five years old, White adults perceive Black boys as threatening. Also, by age five, Black girls experience an adultification bias—the idea that they need less protection and nurturing than their White peers.

These projections and stereotypes have real consequences for young Black children. In one Indiana study, approximately 1 percent of White prekindergarten and kindergarten students were suspended or expelled, but that rate jumped to 5 percent for Black students of the same age. By high school, about 9–13 percent of White students are getting suspended or expelled compared to 25–34 percent of Black students. Hispanics fell in between, with 1.2 percent of prekindergartners/kindergartners and 15–23 percent of high schoolers receiving these punishments.[185] While there is a great deal of concern about the treatment of Black boys in school, Black girls are not exempt from harsh treatment either. Black girls are five times more likely to be suspended and almost three times more likely to encounter the juvenile justice system than White girls.[186]

Unequal teaching and learning resources. Unlike most European and Asian nations, the United States has mostly localized, rather than centralized, its school finance systems. Consequently, socioeconomic status and community assets, factors largely associated with race, yield dramatic variations in a child's access to educational resources, such as skilled teachers, small class size, and quality curriculum. A study published in 2015 found that in Washington, DC, teachers of Black, Hispanic, and Native American students were most likely to have less experience and lower licensure exam scores.[187] That study, as well as work by economist Ronald Ferguson, suggests that teacher performance in state certification exams, experience, and degrees have critical relationships to student learning.[188] Compared to schools for White or more affluent students, schools

ACHIEVEMENT AND DISCIPLINE GAPS IN 2,000 SCHOOL DISTRICTS

"There is growing interest in the relation between the racial achievement gap and the racial discipline gap. However, few studies have examined . . . the extent to which racial discipline gaps are related to racial achievement gaps in Grades 3 through 8 in districts across the United States. . . . We find evidence that districts with larger racial discipline gaps have larger racial achievement gaps (and vice versa). . . . We find robust evidence that the positive association between the Black-White discipline gap and the Black-White achievement gap persists after controlling for a multitude of confounding factors. We also find evidence that the mechanisms connecting achievement to disciplinary outcomes are more salient for Black than White students."[189]

—*Researchers Francis A. Pearman II, F. Chris Curran,*
Benjamin Fisher, and Joseph Gardella

for poor children or children of color have the least funding and fewer teaching and curriculum resources, according to Stanford professor Linda Darling Hammond.[190] In concurrence, in 2019 EdBuild reported that White school districts get $23 billion more than non-White districts and spend $14,000 per student compared to $11,682.[191]

Diminished opportunities to be identified as excelling. Black, Hispanic, and Native American children of color are widely underrepresented in gifted programs, relative to Asian and White students. Compared to White students, Black students are 66 percent less likely to be recommended for gifted programs, and Hispanics 47 percent less likely.[192] "We document that even among students with high standardized test scores, Black students are less likely to be assigned to gifted services in both math and reading, a pattern that persists when controlling for other background factors, such as health and socioeconomic status, and characteristics of classrooms and schools," wrote researchers Jason A. Grissom and Christopher Redding in 2016.[193] Having a teacher of color improved the odds that a child of color would be considered gifted.[194] Especially for children from impoverished environments, matching the race or ethnicity of the teacher and student led to better child outcomes.[195]

The new digital divide is emerging as an additional factor that affects a child's performance. While internet access seems fairly even across groups, the amount of time that children spend looking at screens, and how they use these screens, is now the more relevant marker of advantage and disadvantage—a marker significantly affected by race and family

IS EDUCATION THE GREAT EQUALIZER?

"Education . . . beyond all other devices of human origin, is a great equalizer of conditions of men—the balance wheel of the social machinery."[196]

—Horace Mann, the first prominent advocate for public education, *Twelfth Annual Report to the Secretary of the Massachusetts State Board of Education* (1848)

"Few Americans realize that the US educational system is one of the most unequal in the industrialized world, and that students routinely receive dramatically different learning opportunities based on their social status. . . . The end results of these educational inequalities are increasingly tragic. More than ever before in our nation's history, education is not only the ticket to economic success, but also to basic survival."[197]

—Linda Darling Hammond, Charles E. Ducommun Professor of Education Emeritus at the Stanford Graduate School of Education

With respect to economic and social mobility, "the average effect of education at all levels is to reinforce rather than compensate for the differences associated with family background."[198]

—Isabel Sawhill, The Brookings Institute

structure. As a *New York Times* article stated, "Screens used to be for the elite. Now avoiding them is a status symbol."[199] Journalist Naomi Schaefer Riley warned that the new digital divide is actually variations in time spent on screens—and there, the gap is enormous. The children at the disadvantage are the ones who have *more*, not less, access to screens and those who spend a lot of time on social media and video games.[200]

RIGHTING PAST WRONGS

How can we help all Alpha children reach their full potential in the face of these abundant opportunity equity concerns? Added together, all of these lasting legacies of opportunity inequity paint a distinctive picture of distress that is shaping the overall milieu of Generation Alpha. Beneath the consciousness of many Americans, and in contrast to our democratic ideals, lies a strong and surprising truth: opportunity for *all* of our children lags behind that of other nations, and gaps in opportunity for certain groups of children are endlessly debated but not resolved.

To consider resolution, at a minimum, we collectively might consider the ethics of taking the Hippocratic Oath on behalf of Alpha children: First do no harm. This oath has value when we acknowledge the impact of our actions or inaction, as well as reflect on our intentions. The reality is that opportunities to thrive are intertwined with race and class. Our organizational or national behavior, intentionally or not, has the effect of neglecting or being oblivious to inequities that affect millions of our children. What vows are we prepared to make to Alpha children? How do we transform opportunities for this generation at this point in time—now, while Generation Alpha is either very young or not yet born? As their guardians, how might we change circumstances that hinder their physical, social, emotional, or intellectual health?

Alpha children can't feed, clothe, or educate themselves. Children cannot vote to prepare themselves for the social and economic megatrends that will be the setting of their lives. We know that our country can make different decisions—examples from other nations show us that we can improve the odds that all of our children survive, thrive, and soar in this twenty-first century if different policy decisions are made. Advocacy for our children isn't simply an act of kindness, charity, or goodwill—it serves as an act of justice. Focus on opportunity inequity is in the very best interest of all children who are part of a generation defined by its diversity.

Martin Luther King Jr. drew on an 1853 sermon by the abolitionist minister Theodore Parker when he said, "The arc of the moral universe is long, but it bends toward justice." I agree with King, as I can readily see the progress that has been made over the past decades. But that progress has been slow and difficult.

A 2018 international report estimated that it could take at least five generations or 150 years for impoverished children and families to achieve the average income across OECD countries.[201] At the fiftieth anniversary of the Coleman report, economist and policy analyst Eric Hanushek estimated that at the pace of the previous half-century, it would take two-and-a-half centuries to close the Black-White math achievement gap in the United States and would be more than one-and-a-half centuries until the reading gap closes.[202] The National Institute for Early Education Research reports that at the current rate of growth, it would take twenty years for state preschool programs to have enough seats to enroll half of the nation's four-year-olds.[203]

Clearly, a faster pace of change is warranted. Yet change is complex—and Kuhn reminds us that paradigm shifts take time—because much of what influences the lives of Alpha children happens within the intersection of multiple variables. Children benefit—or are encumbered—by the multiplier effects of family support, early childhood education, and opportunities for achievement. The need for family support cannot be viewed as a completely separate issue from child care or from a child's opportunities for achievement. All of these issues represent multiple interconnected, overlapping, and interdependent systems.

Just as the complexity of change is affected by intersectionality, change also encounters constantly shifting community dynamics. Within broad categories of race, for example, there are intricate layers of dynamic diversity based on social class, citizenship status, skin color, or English language proficiency, for example. Moreover, all ethnic groups that are affected continually evolve, although the narrative of the data about the relative opportunity for any specific cultural group may not have changed much over the decades. In the face of this dynamic complexity, default positions, such as blaming parents or teachers separately for the achievement gap, are too narrow and simplistic to engender respectful, sustainable change.

Yet, as the arc bends toward justice, there is constancy: the protective shield that most Alpha children receive from their families, regardless of their economic circumstances. As attested by countless biographies, sociological analyses, and empirical research, it is families who are at the foundation and core of the children's intersectionality throughout the cycle of their childhoods. And that's why a renewed, authentic and intensive focus on family empowerment and mobilization, and strong, widespread voices for child advocacy are game changers.

STRATEGIES TO ACHIEVE GAME CHANGER #3: OPPORTUNITY EQUITY

With emphasis on families as assets, we need one comprehensive strategy to achieve game changer #3: empower and mobilize the families of Alpha children. It will accomplish two goals:

- Build families' capacity to maximize value from our existing systems.

- Leverage their latent desires for social change into actionable policy that supports Alpha children with more family support and opportunity equity.

These two goals will best be accomplished when we acknowledge the ineffectiveness of our current systems and embrace new paradigms.

OUR CURRENT SYSTEMS ARE INEFFECTIVE

Existing levels of family support and parent engagement are ineffective for virtually all families. Despite consensus about the power of investing in young children, it is an open secret that policies and programs for young children and their families are not working to their optimal potential.

Given the pervasive and persistent depths of inequities in our nation, it would require an inordinate leap of faith to conclude that our existing policies or programs as they are—even with more funding—will set the path for equitable opportunities for Alpha children. But a powerful remedy may be hiding in plain sight: the transformative power of families to make a difference in the lives of Alpha children, especially if this power is collectively leveraged to garner more social policy impact as well.

A focus on the importance of families is not new. In 1966 Coleman's report found decidedly in favor of the family as a major force that governs children's academic development. Likewise, a guiding principle of Head Start has always promoted what was called maximum feasible parent participation. Since the 1980s, "two-generation model" programs have been created on the assumption that simultaneous interventions with parents and children would be more effective than serving each group individually.

While the focus on families is not new, the power of family engagement has never quite been realized. In the politically charged atmosphere of its era, the Coleman report findings were never fully acted upon. In Head Start, the idea of families' maximum feasible participation became associated with civil rights struggles. And, although the idea of two-generation programs is theoretically sound, the early results have not been strong, partly because the adult components in these settings were "not intensive, widely implemented, or extensively studied," as evaluated by researchers.[204]

Nevertheless, experts such as Ron Haskins, Irwin Garfinkel, and Sara McLanahan continually point out that "the school problems of poor children stem in large part from the home environment."[205] As evidence, they cite studies showing that affluent families, relative to the poor, have different home language environments and spend more time with their children in conversation, verbal responsiveness, and literary activities. Yet despite these findings on home environments, their transference to early childhood programs has been challenging due to the lack of clear definitions and measurements.

Yet despite the measurement challenges, both historical and contemporary wisdom continue to give countenance to the potential power parents hold to support their children. Research has demonstrated consistently that the most effective child development programs work with children *and their families.* And, important to note, the oft-cited landmark studies in early childhood education did not consist entirely of an academic program for children. Rather, these very successful programs offered family supports such as home visits and parent education—early learning services that are too rarely included in the current political clamor to establish universal preschool. This is another example of our perennial failure to apply what we know to what we actually do.

EMBRACING NEW PARADIGMS

How can we leverage this potential power of families to achieve opportunity equity? What can we do now to get the best payoff for the entire generation of Alpha kids? How can we help each family and all Alpha children to reach their full potential?

The required paradigm shifts would repair ethical and equity issues and advance universal approaches to serving children, hearing all voices for all children. In one necessary paradigm shift, we must move away from ethical and equity issues that account for the limitations of past efforts. These issues include parent involvement approaches that

- construct restricted roles for families' influence and ability to be productive social actors. *In contrast, programs could host regular community meetings with agendas that emerge from families' questions. Ensure translation services where appropriate. Provide two-way communication options. Involve families in important decisions about the program and their child.*

- assess parents, parenting, and school interactions based on archetypical White middle-class models. *In contrast, surround all families with a sense of welcome in ways that are meaningful to them. Recognize that middle-class White parents can activate their cultural and social capital in order to support their children in ways that may not be comfortable for other parents. Acknowledge that differences in family structure, culture, ethnic background, social class, age, and gender could affect family or educator perceptions of the interactions. Assess your potential biases about these differences. Build on the cultural values of families, emphasizing personal contact. Without judgment, accommodate alternative scheduling of meetings based on employment, translation, or transportation needs to work with families.*

- present barriers to efforts by families to advocate for their children. *Listen to how parents and teachers define the child's needs and how best to address them. Openly discuss divergent perspectives before determining how best to address them.*

- fail to recognize the structural power inequality that exists between parents and the professionals who work with them, specifically the implicit judgment involved when professionals evaluate their "needs." *Instead, focus on collaboration, partnership, and frequent conversation as a means to engage teachers and families with each other, building shared cultural capital.*

A second necessary paradigm shift is the move toward more universal, rather than targeted, change efforts. This paradigm shift rests on two key principles:

- **First: "All voices!"** We must empower and engage **all** families, teachers, and friends of Alpha kids in order to make a difference for the entire generation. Our current family initiatives focus primarily on children with special needs or the poor, who are disproportionately people of color.

- **Second: "For all children!"** Our strategies and solutions must be universally available for all children, not targeted to children of a specific income or background. Solutions must support an entire generation of children through structural change that includes family leave and more equitable program funding.

The drive behind "All voices—for all children" is that the focus must be broad, universal change. Universalism means that all of our Alpha children receive access to benefits such as family leave. Within this universal frame, an equity lens would allow targeted support to achieve greater equality. Universal approaches also recognize that support for our children is a public good that benefits us all. Infant mortality or a child who reads poorly, for example, are not just personal tragedies.

To affect these necessary paradigm shifts, empowerment and engagement strategies might be constructed to answer the following three sets of questions affirmatively.

1. Does the initiative have a philosophy of empowerment which:

- **identifies and focuses on the family's unique assets, strengths, and competence**, rather than starting from questioning what is wrong or different about them.

- **elevates family voices** in their roles as consumers of infant health, social services, and educational opportunities. Creates safe spaces—multiracial, generational, and varied income, where possible—where families' unsaid hopes and desires (latent demand) can be freely expressed, becoming actionable demands for policies and services that benefit their children.

- **values families as partners with professionals.** Family demand and advocacy must become a vital part of any change efforts. The people actually affected by a policy change must have their own equally valued voice, in addition to the voice of specialists. For example, important efforts to "professionalize" services such as early childhood education have been largely driven by the field's experts, which I believe has limited the impact of important changes. Elevate the voices of families themselves, rather than professionals speaking on their behalf.

- **positions families as leaders** so that they become a force for—and the leaders of—change. Empowerment approaches enhance families' sense of attaining control over their lives as well as promoting democratic participation in community life.

2. Does the initiative offer services with dignity and respect which:

- **respects and celebrates family and ethnic cultures or languages**, using them as vehicles for transmitting support.

- **uses family and community initiative as drivers of change.**
  Build policies and programs from the ideas and innovations that
  emerge from within the families and communities themselves.
  Families must cocreate—not only be the recipients of—change.

3. Does the initiative build family advocacy which:

- **enhances capacity.** Service delivery and policy models must
  explicitly seek to increase families' feelings of personal power
  while building their capacity to influence people, organizations,
  and environments affecting their Alpha children.

- **encourages family leadership and action to help their Alpha
  child right now.** Strengthen families' ability to access existing
  or advocate for new resources. Build the skills and capacities of
  parents to speak, act, and make choices or decisions on their
  own behalf rather than expecting professionals to confirm parent
  or child needs. Build parent capacity to maximize value from
  existing systems, leveraging services for their Alpha children who
  cannot wait for large system changes in the limited time that is
  their early childhood.

- **transforms the lives of families by focusing on root-cause
  solutions.** Empowering families also enhances their competency to recognize and respond to systems that affect their lives. A
  focus on solutions requires initiatives to ensure that families gain
  information, real competencies, concrete skills, material resources, genuine opportunities, and tangible results.

- **keeps a generational perspective.** Without a future-based and
  imaginative orientation, change efforts may increase the number
  of silos—that is, stand-alone programs with goals, tools, priorities, and processes that are independent from each other. The
  silo mentality can create counterproductive or conflicting man-
  dates among community, state, and national initiatives. Another
  consequence of a right-now focus is that it tends to emphasize

providing services while neglecting or deprioritizing the root causes of issues such as racism or classism.

Affirmative responses to these questions could help translate the potential of parent engagement into a sense of personal power within families. Often, this sense of personal power must precede political action: the person internalizes a sense of self-efficacy in ways that boost a sense of self-esteem. Once personal power is internalized, it can be assessed, allowing for choice to inspire and influence activities that build on the grassroots activism of families and local stakeholders.

PROGRESS IS POSSIBLE AND PROBABLE

In 1976 Gil Steiner's widely read analysis, *The Children's Cause*, was not optimistic about policy efforts on behalf of children. As Steiner saw it, "children's policy is not successfully nurtured in official conferences, commissions, or advisory committees."[206] We believe Steiner would be amazed to see the considerable progress that has been made in children's policy since the 1970s. Nevertheless, to advance our game changers for Alpha children we recommend much greater levels of family participation as voters and as program or policy activists for children. Efforts to support the collective voice and vote for families could take many forms, including

- mobilizing parents through awareness raising;
- fostering family agency and capacity to confront discrimination, bias, and inequity;
- reducing segregation in children's early childhood education experiences;
- messaging about families' experiences with media campaigns or social media;
- self-organizing efforts at the neighborhood, school, and community levels to advocate for their rights and for the rights of their children;
- facilitating peer learning, collaboration, and networking activities within and between parent groups; and

- including families from all backgrounds on program or municipal governance bodies.

In this way, we, the adults in their lives, work together to build understanding, power, and the will to drive change in the way our current systems operate while simultaneously working to create new systems. Making actionable social demands that families and teachers are ready to fight for will be required to remove the political and policy barriers that today prevent change in family support, economic security, and educational options.

I have already mentioned how our peer countries are moving forward on policies related to family leave, economic security, and equity. Simply importing practices from other countries is unlikely to be effective. But in the process of finding our own way of advancing our society, we must not allow ourselves to remain outside of the international circle of consensus about children's needs and rights, absent some widely accepted rationale. For example, more than thirty years following the United Nations Convention on the Rights of the Child, the most widely and rapidly ratified treaty in history, the United States is the only country in the world that hasn't ratified it. This convention has a widely accepted rationale, and our absence as a signatory puzzles many people within and outside of our nation.

> "Until our nation's parents get organized, American politicians will continue to say, 'Children are our future' without delivering a coherent public policy that honors those words in action."[207]
>
> —Rob Reiner, actor and philanthropist

This book has clearly set out rationales for why parent empowerment, activism, and engagement are critical. The challenge is how such family mobilization might occur and who might participate in it.

In sum, enhancing families' voice and vote is the next best step in promoting the opportunity equity that is urgently needed for all Alpha children in the United States today. In synthesizing everything we know about opportunity equity, it's clear that the time for change—to raise and educate Alpha children with fewer burdens of our unequal past—is now. "All voices! For all children!" **How can we shift the paradigm of families as recipients of change rather than the cocreators of change?**

BOLD
Choosing Possible Futures

For while I take inspiration from the past, like most Americans, I live for the future. . . . Well I've said it before, and I'll say it again—America's best days are yet to come. Our proudest moments are yet to be. Our most glorious achievements are just ahead. America remains what Emerson called her one hundred and fifty years ago, 'the country of tomorrow.' What a wonderful description and how true. . . . More than two centuries later, America remains on a voyage of discovery, a land that has never become, but is always in the act of becoming.[208]

—*President Ronald Reagan*

More than half a century after the Kerner and Coleman reports, the nation's racial demographics have upended the Black-White paradigm that prevailed in 1968. No serious thinking about our national future can now disregard our increased diversity. We recognize that the megatrends encompassing the lives of the Alpha generation will require significant game changers to support their development to be the best they can be. These game changers represent bold signals that our nation "is always in the act of becoming":

- We can no longer indulge in the luxury of attributing different social outcomes to inherent qualities or shortcomings of individuals or groups independent of the social policies and supports that are provided to families. Our nation must rebalance its focus on the difficult challenge of confronting structural obstacles to equity rather than on personal failings.

- We will create a new future for Alpha children, a future that strongly embeds opportunities for all within our strong democratic traditions.

CHOOSING ALTERNATIVE FUTURES: BECOMING BOLD

So how do we begin to choose possible alternative futures? Here we offer five processes or strategies: scenario planning; fact checking; validating the lived experiences of families; engaging multigenerational voices; and deciding to have dialogue and to act with others. In this chapter we also contrast the archetypes of the Fluid Nation and Fixed Nation, sharing broad outlines of the perspectives of each category. Being bold actors on behalf of the Alpha generation will necessarily involve increased citizen mobilization, using an equity lens to focus on the impact of our choices and choosing to transform, rather than conform to, our current national circumstances.

STRATEGY #1: SCENARIO PLANNING

In recent years, scenario-based strategic planning, also called alternative futures planning, outlines best- and worst-case situations in order to forecast or stimulate thinking about choices, trends, and game changers. Although there are many variations of alternative futures planning, they all intend to explore realistic ways in which the future could unfold. Obviously, when it comes to matters related to children, families, race, racial identity, or public policy, there are endless plausible possibilities that might be examined as one considers bold action. Rigorous scenario planning takes into account a vast number of complexities that help you explore the issues and make decisions. While this text does not offer a full engagement of the discipline of real-life scenario planning process, consider this methodology in your community and use the insights gained to move forward. In this way, scenario planning enables you to envision possible futures in view of the megatrends and game changers proposed. The idea is that by using our collective foresight and decision-making powers, we can select from many different paths and possibilities to achieve the game changers.

STRATEGY #2: FACE THE FACTS

Taking an unsentimental look at the facts is a prerequisite to bold action. And, as we have seen, the facts show that the United States ranks at or near the bottom on many indicators of governmental policies toward children and that clear racial disparities lie at the heart of our outcomes for children. America may not be talked about as "Black" and "White" anymore, but the country is still characterized by inequalities that now expand to include the rainbow of ethnicities.

These facts may be news to many Americans, immersed in the notion of American exceptionalism. Yet declining proportions of Americans agree that the United States "stands above all other countries in the world": 38 percent in 2011, 28 percent in 2014, and 24 percent by 2019.[210]

"What does it mean to be bold?"

"The dictionary defines it as 'showing an ability to take risks; confident and courageous.' But I like the thesaurus description much better: daring, intrepid, brave, valiant, valorous, fearless, dauntless, audacious, adventurous, heroic, plucky, spirited, confident, assured, swashbuckling . . .

"The opposite approach is to be timid. And who wants to be known as bashful, fearful, apprehensive, timorous, trepid, intimidated, mousy, cowardly, faint-hearted, pusillanimous, or wimpy . . .

"The time to be bold is now! Being timid is not a goal or desired state, it is a default when we don't pause and get it right, make it big, and stay focused on achieving something!"[209]

—*Holly Green, CEO and Managing Director of The Human Factor, Inc.*

Jay Ogilvy, co-founder of the Global Business Network of scenario planners, outlines one possible scenario planning process as follows:

Step 1: Focal issue: Identify what a person or organization will focus on.

Step 2: Key factors: Brainstorm factors that could affect the focal issue.

Step 3: External forces: Consider and creatively imagine the impact of remote forces.

Step 4: Critical uncertainties: Prioritize.

Step 5: Scenario logics: Select ideas about which to prepare detailed scenarios.

Step 6: Scenarios: Craft the story of each chosen scenario into just one clear narrative line.

Step 7: Implications and options: Ascertain scenario implications and the strategic choices that would follow.

Step 8: Early indicators: Watch for signs of scenario evolution and begin implementing the strategy related to that scenario.[211]

The older you are, the more likely you are to hold positive views: the Pew Research Center reports that within the Silent generation, it is the oldest members who feel most strongly about America's greatness, as fully 72 percent of those aged seventy-six to eighty-three said the United States is the greatest country in the world. In contrast, only 32 percent of Millennials said that the United States is the greatest. Pew observes that, among older adults, there is a tension between their belief that America is the greatest country in the world and a sense of pessimism about the country's future. In contrast, young Americans are more optimistic about the nation's current path although less persuaded of the greatness of our nation.[212]

Honoring our nation's historic successes is not diminished by recognition of its shortfalls, whether they are within our nation or happening internationally. Our national success factors—such as the sense of freedom experienced by most Americans, along with our work ethic—are cornerstones from which we can build a more equitable and inclusive society for Generation Alpha. More, we can ill afford to stay silent about the realities of life for our youngest children. Acknowledging the diversity of our nation today, and in the spirit of patriotism, it is honorable for the teachers and families of the Alpha generation to ask the emperor to try on new clothes!

Along with the new clothes we might develop both a more humble— and yet stronger—view of ourselves and our nation's role in the world. As Americans, we look at the facts and realistically come to terms with the notion that our present circumstances, and possibly our children's futures, are less exceptional than once imagined.

But we also know that these circumstances and facts can be changed. We must first face them and relinquish complacency, a silent killer of the instinct to act. Becoming bold means facing the facts realistically, letting go of false or hoped-for narratives about realities. We will open Pandora's box—and we will find hope inside.

STRATEGY #3: VALIDATING COGNITIVE DISSONANCE AND OUR LIVED EXPERIENCES

When we consider the facts, we see clearly a growing gap between our current national paradigms and the typical lived experiences of many families. We begin to recognize that other countries have made different policy choices than we have, with different results for family life. In child care, for example, we have relied on market forces to arbitrate price and quality. We can now see that such reliance, no matter how well intended, has not produced equity of opportunity for either young children or their parents, especially mothers.

When we notice the gap between our ideologies and our actual lives, that's when we begin to recognize, understand, and experience cognitive dissonance. Our cultural frameworks have taught us well that we should

> **cognitive dissonance:**
>
> The state of having inconsistent thoughts, beliefs, or attitudes, especially as relating to behavioral decisions and attitude change.
>
> —*Lexico*

be self-made individuals, achieving the good life based on our merit. But we also sense that, in today's interdependent America, these ideologies can create a senseless feeling of failure. This ethos exacerbates loneliness and alienation, especially if we lack family social supports, experience poverty with our children, or cannot afford the preschool we desire for our child. John Dickinson, a delegate to the Continental Congress, noted as far back as 1768 that "a people is travelling fast to destruction, when individuals consider their interests as distinct from those of the public."[213] We need a Declaration of Interdependence!

STRATEGY #4: VALUING MULTIGENERATIONAL VOICES

Millennials—the "woke," or socially conscious, generation that largely parents Generation Alpha—have often taken up the call for social equality and equal rights regardless of race, sexual orientation, religion, or gender. These values are expressed through priorities such as wellness, environmental sustainability, and global consciousness and activism. The new "woke" generation is calling for a pluralistic rainbow of leadership from the grass roots to be change agents.

Indeed, many voices will be required for change. Change agents must be able to connect the dots between many generations, between parents and nonparents, between teachers and other professions, and across cultures. Each of these groups brings the interdependent talents, skills, and unique perspectives or experiences required to build relevant, accountable, trusting connections that will accommodate the needs of our children and the demographic shifts they represent. Interactions among multiple generations increase opportunities for learning, growth, innovation, entrepreneurial thinking, authenticity, respect—and wisdom. Becoming bold means being a courageous visionary—even a disruptive innovator—who is not afraid to speak up and change the conversation, encourage fresh thinking, and introduce new ideas, ideals, and thought-provoking dialogue. We welcome and value multigenerational voices since these times of cultural transition must call forth numerous leaders who see our nation through an equity lens rather than relying on formal, centralized control. Collaboration across generations will be essential to move forward toward equity as well as to reach agreement about and implement the game changers.

STRATEGY #5: DISCUSSING ALTERNATIVE FUTURES

For the Alpha generation, we will be asked to create safety nets and social networks that will benefit us all collectively rather than engaging in our individual family child care or family leave struggles. We will therefore have a lot of thought-provoking ideas to discuss! Possible futures must consider nothing less than

- how multigenerational and new voices will be heard;
- how to rally Americans to help our society accommodate

DISRUPTIVE INNOVATORS

"As a pivotal force for change, to disrupt does not mean to break something but to recognize that something is already broken and needs new ideas and unprecedented innovation: ideas that no one, anywhere, at any time, have thought of before. As efficient problem-solvers, disruptive innovators distinguish themselves by crafting and delivering better ways of achieving a goal, of building a better mousetrap. But they do not disrupt simply for the sake of change or creating commotion. They do it to fill gaps, to do what others can't or won't do."[214]

—The New Early Childhood Professional: A Step-by-Step Guide to Overcoming Goliath, *by Valora Washington, Brenda Gadson, and Kathryn L. Amel* the inevitable social and economic transition that is already upon us; and

- how to adapt to shifting values as people reconsider what are reasonable or rational policies in our new circumstances.

Ready or not, when it comes to the Alpha generation, culture change is imminent. For some, this change as embodied in the megatrends is unwelcome and undesirable. For others, the game changers we envision will offer welcomed and desirable relief.

No matter which type of alternative future you might prefer, many of us will come to the realization that political processes must be engaged if we are to achieve systematic change in our complex society. New public choices seem possible, even as we also recommend that families work to maximize value from existing systems to serve their Alpha children's right-now needs. As multigenerational coalitions attain more critical mass, the political process begins and eventually ratifies the cultural change that actually has already taken place as a new social reality.

"Only very wealthy people can afford current decent care and education [for young children] . . . . Very few can afford what we estimate is the cost of quality care."[215]

—*Richard Brandon, coauthor of a 2018 report on early education financing from the National Academies of Sciences, Engineering, and Medicine*

"From age 0 to age 5 we say, 'Parents, you're on your own,' and then at age 5, we start child care and education, even though we know from child development how much happens from birth to age 5."[216]

—*Elliot Haspel, author of* Crawling Behind: America's Child Care Crisis and How to Fix It

ARCHETYPES AND PERSPECTIVES

As we move forward together as a nation, we can imagine at least two alternative futures

> "We cannot afford to postpone investing in children until they become adults, nor can we wait until they reach school age—a time when it may be too late to intervene."[217]
>
> *—Nobel prize–winning economist James Heckman, reporting a permanent boost in IQ for children followed for more than thirty-five years after experiencing high-quality early childhood education*

for culture change: A Fixed Nation that more slowly adapts to—or works to reframe and rebut—the game changers or a Fluid Nation that adapts more rapidly and works to implement them. Of course, there are many more possibilities in between. But these two scenarios offer broad perspectives from which we might begin. And begin we must!

Borrowing from an analysis by Stacie Goffin and myself[218] about the leadership choices in early childhood education, I outline four approaches that Fixed or Fluid Nation adherents might use to make decisions about the way forward for the Alpha generation:

- Fixed Nation adherents are likely to be guardians, who protect historically valued positions, or accommodators, who work to maintain equilibrium.

- Fluid Nation adherents are likely to be entrepreneurs, who pursue the nation's new realities as strategic opportunities to secure improvements, or architects, who focus on conditions that can promote sustainable results.

These two archetypes represent divergent perspectives, and obviously there are many

ARCHETYPES

An archetype is a universal symbol or idea. Psychologist Carl Jung understood archetypes as a collectively inherited unconscious idea, pattern of thought, image, and so forth, universally present in individual psyches.

ARCHETYPES

	FIXED NATION		
	GUARDIANS	*ACCOMMODATORS*	
WORLDVIEW	Protective	Realistic	
MOTIVATING FACTOR	Consistency; stability	Maintaining equilibrium; realism	
APPROACH TO CHANGE	Wary; grounded in history	Pragmatic; consensus building	
ACTION ORIENTATION	Cautious; interested in sustaining historical values	Incremental; moves to the "middle" to create new mainstream	
PRIMARY APPROACH TO RAISING ALPHA CHILDREN	Protects traditional views of children and their growth	Sensitive to ideas at the center of traditional and emerging viewpoints	
PRIMARY SLANT FOR THINKING ABOUT FAMILY SUPPORT	Protects the nation's traditional, charitable mission to support children and families	Sensitive to the nation's traditional, charitable mission to support children and families when adjusting to contemporary context	
PRIMARY SLANT FOR THINKING ABOUT ADULT RESPONSIBILITY FOR GENERATION ALPHA	Protects the child and his or her development	Sensitive to the interface between child's development and public expectations	

FLUID NATION	
ENTREPRENEURS	*ARCHITECTS*
Opportunistic	Holistic
Strategic improvements; competitive advantage	Catalyzing change through effective policy
Welcoming and anticipatory	Long-term view; focused on creating conditions for sustainable results
Results-oriented	Future-oriented; proactive
Pursues new frames of reference that will promote innovative opportunities	Seeks hidden potential that can promote new commitments to children
Pursues new thinking in order to expand horizons and future possibilities	Seeks essential/core elements that promote resilience in changing circumstances
Responds to public opinion	Seeks alignment between intentions and results; equity lens

gradients of possibilities that could lie ahead. The Fixed Nation and the Fluid Nation are used here to illustrate two potentialities—potentialities that are intentionally stark to distinguish between them.[219] Moreover, any individual or group may use more than one decision-making approach; depending on the context, any of the approaches has the potential for positive or negative outcomes.

ALTERNATIVE FUTURES: CHANGING CONTEXTS

There is more than one approach to "the country of tomorrow." In a nation as vast as ours, many perspectives will present themselves, and achieving consensus will be challenging. Demography is NOT necessarily destiny, so an increase in the number of Alpha children of color will not automatically yield increasing social justice for them or harmony among us all.

In a Fixed Nation or Fluid Nation scenario, alternative futures depict a nation that changes—the difference is whether it changes relatively slowly and reluctantly or more rapidly and enthusiastically. Archetypical guardians, accommodators, entrepreneurs, or architects will exhibit characteristic attitudes, behaviors, and differences of opinion that may illustrate their approaches. In the table on pages 118–119, we provide examples of these divergent perspectives by presenting what might be the dominant world views of a Fixed or Fluid Nation.

BEING BOLD

One of the most important things that adults can do for the Alpha generation is to bring greater intentionality to the choices we make that will affect their futures. We must consider alternatives such as the Fixed Nation or Fluid Nation and all the choices in between. Talking with people who have divergent experiences and opinions will reveal more clearly the challenges and opportunities available to us as a nation.

In essence, being bold will require greater levels of citizen engagement and mobilization; a clear focus on the impact rather than the intentions of our policies and programs, using tools such as an equity lens; and deciding to transform, rather than conform to, our current national circumstances.

BEING BOLD: CITIZEN ENGAGEMENT AND MOBILIZATION

What do Americans prefer after hearing Fixed Nation perspectives contrasted with the Fluid Nation ideas that are presented in this book? Are Americans ready to advocate for and attain the game changers in family support, early childhood education, and opportunity equity?

I think so! A wide range of voters, Democrats (90 percent), Independents (70 percent), and Republicans (70 percent), express support for expanded early childhood education funding.[220] Americans agree by wide margins—two-thirds—that both business and government should do more to support working parents by funding child care.[221] Eighty-two percent support paid leave for mothers, 69 percent support paid paternity leave, 85 percent support paid leave for workers dealing with their own serious health condition, and 67 percent support paid leave for those caring for a family member who is seriously ill.[222]

However, saying "yes" or "no" in an opinion poll is a very different phenomena than taking specific action toward change. Citizen engagement and mobilization is a key and underdeveloped factor in attaining the proposed game changers. Greater citizen engagement and mobilization would represent a deepened sense of urgency and rising energy for change.

"The health of a democratic society may be measured by the quality of functions performed by private citizens."

—Alexis de Tocqueville, ca. 1835

FIXED NATION AND FLUID NATION PERSPECTIVES

ATTITUDES

FIXED NATION	FLUID NATION
Experiences anxiety, fear, threat, loss, or anger about demographic change, shifting both their racial and political attitudes to become more conservative on a variety of policies, whether race-related or not.	Celebrates and welcomes demographic change as means to strengthen the nation's range of talent and influence; more liberal on a variety of policies, whether race-related or not.
Perpetuates myths and stereotypes about various ethnic groups, including their own.	Explores and learns from human diversity.
Dismisses nonprofit organizations and citizen coalitions as secondary to government or corporate power.	Promotes private-public partnerships.
Self-interest motivates behavior.	Common good motivates behavior.
Persistent focus on the complexities of issues stalls forward movement.	A focus on the principles of issues propels movement.

BEHAVIORS

FIXED NATION	FLUID NATION
Racializes public health events—a behavior that continues a pronounced historic legacy through isolating behaviors, commentary, or joking about specific groups.	Questions the relevance of linking public health to race unless it is solution oriented.
"Celebrates" cultures primarily through narratives that focus on their oppression (enslavement).	Balances and humanizes cultural experiences through their collective civic engagement, resistance efforts, literature, intersectional identities, or liberation struggles.
Marginalizes those perceived as others in ways such as mispronouncing unfamiliar names, generating nicknames for others, and expressing disapproval of social change.	Uses differences as opportunities for learning about the history, origin, or family connotations of certain names.
Practices discrimination related to differences such as hairstyles or food choices, often through microaggression rather than overt behaviors.	Expresses interest, curiosity, or openness when exposed to new ways of being.

HANDLING DIFFERENCES OF OPINION

FIXED NATION	FLUID NATION
Avoids or postpones deliberation of game changers.	Seeks dialogue.
Prefers private-sector decisions over government involvement in employment policies.	Promotes government as a partner with the private sector.
Projects fears of backlash or negative outcomes if game changers such as family leave are introduced. Fears employers will become less willing to hire women of childbearing age.	Anticipates family benefits and champions positive outcomes.
Questions the relevance of comparing US policies to what the rest of the world is doing.	Values and learns from international comparisons.
Advocates for family "choice."	Advocates for the expansion of system choices.
Debates the value of game changers for its demographic.	Assesses benefits for all children.
Focuses on children's needs/means testing.	Promotes all children's rights.
Emphasizes the cost, feasibility, or efficiency of change rather than benefits.	Emphasizes the benefits over costs and the need for difficult political choices.
Focuses on the ambiguities or inconclusiveness of research in order to raise doubts about moving forward.	Focuses on research synthesis.
Minimizes practitioner voice or family experience as unreliable or unscientific.	Highlights family and practitioner wisdom.

LIKELY OUTCOMES FOR THE ALPHA GENERATION

FIXED NATION	FLUID NATION
Generates increases in "externalities"—unanticipated social costs—such as widening racial achievement gaps or reverse gains in maternal employment.	Generates an increase in experimentation and innovation, for example, to close achievement gaps.
Shrinks our public resource base, making public-private partnerships that value caring more difficult.	Expands access to public resources and reduces income inequality.
Reduces our capacity to respond if automation creates massive job loss or reduction in work hours, reducing a family's need for child care.	Explores alternatives to traditional work and family life.
Conforms to the existing social welfare systems to address needs or to receive financial support.	Transforms the existing social welfare systems to address equity needs, including financial adjustments.
Less optimistic for the future.	More optimistic about the future.
American influence/wealth growing.	American influence/wealth waning.
Focus of concern is the degradation of American moral values.	Focus on appreciation of the diversity and complexity of change in American moral values.

How is citizen engagement and mobilization ignited? Often individuals and communities perceive discrepancies between their circumstances and their values or goals. An energetic response to this perception occurs when people coalesce into informal groups and networks to explore those discrepancies. Both a strength and challenge of these informal groups and networks is that dialogue often occurs in settings that are participatory, flexible, cooperative, organic, and integrative expressions of their aspirations. These networks often do not have formal headquarters, leaders, or decision-making hierarchy. They are created and self-organized by the mutual attraction of individuals who share similar values and worldviews.

> "Democracy becomes a functional necessity whenever a social system is competing for survival under conditions of chronic change."[223]
>
> —Warren Bennis, author and pioneer in the field of leadership studies

They are sustained by the desire to share ideas and knowledge in emotionally safe settings. In the process, people and groups become allies and create opportunities to develop coalitions.

Citizen voice and expression have without question been amplified by social media and other uses of technology. Through Facebook, Twitter, and other media, these networks can now create national events, amplify consumer demand, and demonstrate grassroots interest in a social issue in a matter of hours. New technologies can shift the roles of citizen and government, affording individuals and groups unprecedented capabilities to organize and collaborate in new ways around shared ideas in the virtual world as well as carry out sustained action. A challenge of the use of these technologies, however, is that they can also be used to swiftly disseminate misinformation or narrow public perspectives rather than broaden them.

BEING BOLD: USING AN EQUITY LENS

For many years, the child advocacy group Zero to Three has organized "Strolling Thunder," a national event in which hundreds of parents, babies, and advocates from all over the country visit Capitol Hill to call on Congress to make babies a national priority. With Strolling Thunder and myriad other events, parents and their allies have tremendous potential to influence public policy. It's a case in point, a resounding "Yes!" to the idea that we as citizens can create conditions of opportunity for all of our children, with a focus on equity and shoring up social safety nets for particularly vulnerable children, such as children of color, dual-language learners, and the poor. How will we know when there is greater equity? Inequity is quite evident when we can predict the children's outcomes based on demographic factors such as race, gender, the language spoken at home, or physical abilities. When our ability to predict typical results is no longer tied to those factors, equity will exist. Let me explain further.

One strategy being used today to unlink demography and destiny is the equity lens. At its core, an equity lens is a way of paying focused attention to race, ethnicity, and other barriers when analyzing the differential impact (*not* intentions) of public policies. It is an attempt to level the playing field by engaging in reflective questions and processes that deconstruct what is not working and explicitly focus on solutions. Although people often think of "equality" and "equity" as synonyms, they are not. A focus on racial equity is bold because it

- values fair and just distribution of resources and opportunities for individuals and groups;
- courageously commits to unearthing root causes of differential impact;
- engages communities in planning, decision making, and evaluation, ensuring that the people affected by the policies are represented; and
- addresses barriers to racial equity in and between individuals, institutions, and systems.

BEING BOLD: CHOOSING TO TRANSFORM, NOT JUST CONFORM

Striving for alternative futures requires more of us to be willing to step forward on the front line to seek game changers. It also requires recognition that, under any scenario, life in the United States can never be stagnant. It is constantly affected by economic, international, and other unstable or unpredictable factors, such as a pandemic. Therefore, choosing to transform, rather than conform to, our child-serving systems is not an exercise in making crystal-ball predictions. Rather it is an exercise in exploring the factors that will set the Alpha generation apart from those who came before, based on current and emerging trends.

Of course, there are still countless unknown factors about the developmental significance of the megatrends Generation Alpha children face as they grow up. Uncertainties abound. What happens as our racial identity as a nation alters dramatically? When technology use advances rapidly? Or if adults demonstrate a stronger appetite for citizen mobilization? Maybe, for now, many of us simply choose to conform to the ways things are, unsure about how or whether to realize our capacity to transform the communities in which we live.

Yet the megatrends our children face increase the odds that we are now living—and will continue to live—in a significantly transformative era subject to many possible futures, both fixed and fluid. We can also be sure that we—the adults in the lives of the Alpha generation—have agency to make a difference in what their collective future holds. Clearly there are momentous, historic changes underway. It is the fact of rapid change that makes it difficult to forecast the future of our Alpha children. The former nation in which my Boomer generation grew up is long gone—but the Alpha world is just now emerging.

Take a deeper look at our choices: Will we choose to recognize that our questions about families have forever changed? Will we choose to buy in and to join with others to explore questions for which there are no preexisting answers? To what

> "The American dream is not a sprint, or even a marathon, but a relay. Our families don't always cross the finish line in the span of one generation. But each generation passes on to the next the fruits of their labor."[224]
>
> —*San Antonio Mayor Julian Castro*

extent will our nation choose greater policy synergy regarding family life, in contrast to our current array of public and private approaches that operate in parallel but rarely in concert? And how could such synergy become a foundational driver of our national accountability, data gathering, funding, and governance efforts on behalf of young children?

Choosing to transform—and not just conform—requires an enormous amount of respect for the unknown and for the children who are at the center of change. Transformational efforts that create alternative futures require

- the passage of the time required to build both consensus and to design new systems;

- the creation of new administrative structures and social organization;

POLITICIANS' EARLY CHILDHOOD EDUCATION PROMISES MUST BE FULFILLED

Early childhood education is a popular topic in today's political landscape. A number of politicians have become advocates, including Colorado's Jared Polis, Boston mayor Martin J. Walsh, and New York's Bill de Blasio, promising to establish universal preschool. Specific strategic proposals are often comprehensive, as Michigan's Gretchen Whitmer pledged to prioritize "the first one thousand days of a child's life" with full-day preschool, expanded eligibility for child care subsidies, and increase provider reimbursement rates. The messages from politicians clearly reflect both understanding of the value of early childhood education and a commitment to equity. Detroit mayor Mike Duggan envisions a universal pre-K program because "the challenge of kindergarten readiness is perhaps nowhere more acute than it is in Detroit." California's Gavin Newsom vowed to invest $500 million because "all children, not just the children of a governor or a filmmaker, should have the good life in California."[225]

- an understanding of a multiplicity of possible approaches and their trade-offs;

- broad engagement of people, especially the families and teachers of young children;

- democratic, representative, and distributed power with shared leadership, as new technologies may shift the roles of citizen and state;

- a less contentious and more conciliatory ideologic mindset among the diverse communities within the United States; and

- sensitive management of intensifying interaction between traditional political, religious, and cultural norms and the megatrends of diversity.

For the sake of the Alpha children, let's get started as bold agents of change right now.

HOPEFUL

Faith That We Will Do the Right Thing for the Alpha Generation

Your children are not your children.

They are the sons and daughters of Life's longing for itself.

They come through you but not from you,

And though they are with you yet they belong not to you.

You may give them your love but not your thoughts,

For they have their own thoughts.

You may house their bodies but not their souls,

For their souls dwell in the house of tomorrow, which you cannot visit, not even in your dreams.

You may strive to be like them, but seek not to make them like you.

For life goes not backward nor tarries with yesterday.

You are the bows from which your children as living arrows are sent forth.

The archer sees the mark upon the path of the infinite, and He bends you with His might that His arrows may go swift and far.

Let your bending in the archer's hand be for gladness;

For even as He loves the arrow that flies, so He loves also the bow that is stable.

—Kahlil Gibran

In the twenty-first century, novel technologies, new ways of getting information, and the growth of different cultural groups together demand innovative approaches to help our children thrive.

The Alpha generation represents change, so we teachers and families must adapt the ways we support and educate our youngest children. As the millennium marches on, progress will take place faster than ever before—and our hope is that our children will go "swift and far" in ways we can only imagine.

Many of the children born in 2010 will still be alive in 2100. As Margaret Mead observed, "In the modern world we have invented ways of speeding up invention, and people's lives change so fast that a person is born into one kind of world, grows up in another, and by the time his children are growing up, lives in still a different world."[226] Every parent and teacher knows that, as Gibran wrote, "life goes not backward nor tarries with yesterday." We also realize that the ability to see "the mark upon the path of the infinite" is quite a demonstration of foresight.

In between "yesterday" and the "infinite," each of us adults performs our roles for the Alpha generation expectantly and hopefully. We acknowledge megatrends that reasonably forecast inevitable demographic shifts, for example. Nevertheless, we are empowered by our human agency to give meaning to these trends. We know that our capacity to transform the present world can lift the sights of our children as we teach them to fly. Demography need not determine destiny in the "house of tomorrow." That is our hope. And as Americans, boundless optimism is practically our trademark.

A NATIONAL LEGACY OF HOPE

Limitless optimism—hope and belief in our capacity to be self-actualizing—has been an enduring driving force behind the quest for the American Dream. Hope that each new generation will succeed more than the last is part of our national heritage, a recognizable element in the American DNA.

Both Alexis de Tocqueville, a French observer of American life in the nineteenth century, and Irish philosopher Charles Handy, who retraced de Tocqueville's journey across the nation in 2001, observed that typical Americans, in contrast to the cynicism of Europe, were energetic, enthusiastic, confident, and optimistic about the future. Handy concluded:

"Most Americans seem to believe that the future can be better, and that they are responsible for doing their best to make it that way."[227]

Whether or not Handy's and de Tocqueville's observations still ring true in today's America, we nevertheless contend that the national legacy of hope is not just a stereotype. Throughout war, recession, and the 9/11 tragedy many Americans continued to express hopefulness.

Even in 2019,

- Americans were four times more likely to say that the American Dream is "alive and well" for them personally (27 percent) than say that the American dream is "dead" (7 percent). Still, many Americans expressed caution as two-thirds acknowledged that the Dream is under severe or moderate stress.[228]

- The majority of the top 1 percent of income earners say they've achieved the American Dream, and majorities of low- and middle-income people believe they can still reach it.[229]

- There was clear agreement among the income groups that hard work is seen as very important in being economically successful in the United States today. This agreement persists despite the realities that economic mobility is closely tied to factors external to the person's willingness to work such as race, ethnicity, family income, and neighborhood.

This hopeful and optimistic state of mind has been the unmistakable persona of the American way. It is the engine that has made the United States respected for its scientific and technological innovations, strong international leadership, and legendary entrepreneurial industriousness. President John Kennedy tapped into the American psyche brilliantly when he said, "The vows of this nation can only be fulfilled if we in this nation are first, and, therefore, we intend to be first. . . . We choose to go to the moon in this decade and do the other things, not because they are easy, but because they are hard, because that goal will serve to organize and measure the best of our energies and skills, because that challenge is one that we are willing to accept, one we are unwilling to postpone, and one which we intend to win, and the others, too."[230]

A HOPE DEFICIT?

> "Hope is what led a band of colonists to rise up against an empire. What led the greatest of generations to free a continent and heal a nation. What led young women and young men to sit at lunch counters and brave fire hoses and march through Selma and Montgomery for freedom's cause.
>
> Hope is what led me here today. With a father from Kenya, a mother from Kansas, and a story that could only happen in the United States of America.
>
> Hope is the bedrock of this nation. The belief that our destiny will not be written for us, but by us, by all those men and women who are not content to settle for the world as it is, who have courage to remake the world as it should be."[231]
>
> —*Barack Obama*

Yet, within our contemporary society, that Tocquevillian optimism seems to be dimming. This book is being written in the year 2020—an epic year that is dramatically changing our lives with unprecedented turbulence: intense political strife, massive unemployment, the global pandemic, business collapse, widespread population quarantines, and the Black Lives Matter movement. While the durability and longer-term impact of 2020 circumstances may be unknown, it is clear that deep concerns about our nation have been building for a long time. Indeed, opinion polls over the past decade point to a "hope deficit," a term I define as:

- a wavering confidence that each generation can work its way up in the world and have a better life than the previous generation, and
- faltering certainty that our nation is on the right track.

As hope recedes, our personal happiness does too. Research on happiness trends reveal three clear findings about the emotions of adults in the United States: we have been less happy since 2000;[232]

citizens of many other countries feel happier than we do (we rank about nineteenth in happiness compared to Finland, the most satisfied country, followed by Denmark, Norway, Iceland, and the Netherlands);[233] and the rich are happier with their lives than the poor.[234]

Not surprisingly, a 2019 poll on income inequality found that wealthy people perceive that they have attained the American Dream, and they show little anxiety about the future. At the same time, at all income levels, parents and grandparents felt confident that the American Dream was still possible for their children and grandchildren. This National Public Radio study on income equality noted that these views stood in contrast to the realities of peoples' lives.[235]

These poll results are not unanimous, however. In 2019, a Real Clear Politics poll found that only 23 percent of Boomers and the Silent generation felt that the American Dream was possible for them, and even fewer—15 percent—felt the American Dream is still possible for the next generation.[236] These views are quite decidedly pessimistic. Indeed, a series of opinion poll data since the beginning of the millennium has tracked a steady downhill descent in the proportion of adults who predict that youth will have a better life than their parents:

- 2001: 71 percent of poll respondents said American youth would have a better life than their parents.

- 2008: 66 percent felt that a better life was likely.

- 2010: Half of respondents expected that youth would have a better life than their parents.

- 2011: Only 44 percent of Americans felt optimistic that youth's quality of life would exceed that of their parents. Additionally, hope for the future dropped considerably among both the elderly and wealthier Americans (a contrast to 2008).[237]

- 2017: Only 37 percent of Americans believed that children would grow up to be better off than their parents were financially, a sentiment unchanged since 2013.[238]

"It is very hard for people to thrive when health-care, housing and education costs are so high," said David Grasso, the editor of GenFKD, an education and economy advocacy group for Millennials. "Those are three realities threatening the ability for present and future generations to thrive."[239]

In a separate 2019 poll, 56 percent of Americans expressed optimism about our nation's future. But serious concerns also emerged as Americans expressed worry about a shrinking middle class, economic downturns, income inequalities, divisive partisanship, our moral compass, and the difficulties of life for children, families, and the elderly. Interesting is the fact that this survey found Blacks (70 percent), Hispanics (66 percent), and high school graduates (60 percent) were more optimistic than Whites (51 percent) or college graduates (43 percent).[240]

DEMOGRAPHY: A CHALLENGE TO HOPE

These opinion poll data declines suggest that many Americans now find it more difficult, more challenging, to have hope. These results imply that we are raising Alpha children in a less optimistic era.

Yet it is the very diversity that defines the Alpha generation that emerges as a significant worry related to the hope deficit. When considering the predicted diversity of our nation, that Blacks, Hispanics, and Asians will be a majority by 2050, Pew Research Surveys from 2019 point to several themes:

- **We are cautious about the value of this diversity.** Our collective mind has not clearly concluded whether the new diversity will be good for our nation (35 percent), neither good nor bad (42 percent), or decidedly bad (23 percent).

- **Our views are linked to our own race and ethnicity.** Negative views about shifting demographics are expressed by 28 percent of Whites, 13 percent of Blacks, and 12 percent of Hispanics.

- **We are nervous about the impact of diversity on the customs and values of our nation.** Only 30 percent of Americans believe that the changing population will strengthen our customs and values. And, again, our views are linked to our own racial identity: 46 percent of Whites, 25 percent of Latinos, and 18 percent of

Blacks feel that a majority nation of people of color would weaken American customs and values.

- **And we are apprehensive about how we will all get along.** About half of Americans—49 percent—anticipate similar or increasing levels of racial and ethnic conflict as a result of demographic change.[241]

HOPE REIGNITED BY LESSONS LEARNED

There is no question that dramatic demographic shifts and other Alpha generation megatrends can create a sense of uncertainty for some of us who are adults right now. Significant and rapid evolutions in family compositions or technology, for example, might cause anyone to feel a sense of impending doom. Worries and skepticism are one way we might manage our expectations or concerns about what flies out of Pandora's box.

HOPE REMAINS IN PANDORA'S BOX

The moral of Pandora's Box is that unrestrained curiosity can be dangerous—but hope remained in Pandora's box after everything else flew out. There are numerous interpretations of why hope remained, some of which suggest that hope is sinister because it only prolongs unrealistic expectations.

In my view, hope remaining symbolizes expectations for good things, even in the midst of challenging distractions. Hope is an attitude—a disposition—that leads us to take action rather than to give in to discouragement. Hope implies that our choices matter and that we can influence the direction of events that shape our lives. We are not helpless in the face of unexpected or unforeseen events. Our proactive and positive energy sustains our inner belief that change can and will occur. In the end, we need hope.

As despairing as unprecedented change might sometimes feel, the great strength of this country is our resilience. Yes! There is hope inside Pandora's box . . . and hope has its own power for renewal. As Americans, we bounce back. We remember that we have changed in the past. We will change again. And we already are changing now. Hope can bring unity of purpose—we change together for the sake of our Alpha children. And this hope and optimism can ignite our personal, familial, and professional growth.

Reigniting hope is also a demonstrated part of our national legacy. The United States has displayed enormous capacity to change in the past. Indeed, reinventing ourselves to accommodate changing circumstances is perhaps what the United States has done best in its relatively young history. As President Bill Clinton once remarked, "There is nothing wrong with America that cannot be cured by what is right with America."[242] Indeed, hope finds the irony or humor (depending on your mood) in a nation that has moved from authorizing segregation to rebranding the civil rights struggle as an idea that was practically government organized and embraced by multiple corporate sponsors!

GRANDPARENTS SAY THEY ARE READY FOR THE NEW DIVERSITY

As examples of change that supports Alpha children, witness the growing number of grandparents who have grandchildren of a different or mixed race: 34 percent have grandchildren of a different race or ethnicity. The American Association of Retired Persons (AARP) found that grandparents are embracing multiculturalism and say that it is important that their different-race grandchild knows about both the heritage they share and the heritage they do not share. These accepting attitudes also extend to grandchildren's diverse sexual preferences and gender identities.[243]

Now more than ever, it's important that we learn lessons from the past so we don't repeat the same mistakes. And when we look at inter-group interactions in our country, there are countless times when we have overcome horrific challenges. Our history is also littered with incomplete and unfulfilled reconciliations from which we might learn. Through the suffering, foresight, and action of many everyday heroes, our nation has navigated heart-wrenching challenges before. We have moved from en-slavement to emancipation; created public education for all, dismantling a system that educated only the children of White male landowners; and erased Jim Crow laws to expand voting rights, even electing a Black male president of the United States. These victories have been hard-won strug-gles in the face of racially motivated legal exclusions and illegal appropri-ations of property, life, and liberty. For example, in *The Making of Asian America*, Erika Lee cites the internment of one hundred twenty thousand Japanese-Americans—two thirds of them U.S. citizens.

History is prologue for the Alpha generation. We will bequeath to our children an imperfect nation in which there are racially defined mass incarcerations, Alpha generation contemporaries detained in im-migration camps, and persistent inequities that characterize our system of public education. Healing from historical missteps is incomplete—and full recovery may never be achieved—without justice defined as restoration, reparations, and restitution.

> "We have always held to the hope, the belief, the conviction that there is a better life, a better world, beyond the horizon."[244]
>
> —*President Franklin Delano Roosevelt, 1940*

Still . . . there is hope. In the context of human and civil rights abuses in our past and present, hope insists that the arc bends to-ward justice—and hope can be infinite.

And, hope knows that, through citizen mobilization and action, we have the tools and strength to move forward to bring stronger voice, rep-resentation, and equity for the next generation. To the Alpha generation we also bequeath a legacy of progress.

STRATEGIES TO FILL ALPHA CHILDREN WITH HOPE

We have seen that the Generation Alpha megatrends—and especially the demographic shifts—raise many questions for us as the adults responsible for our children's well-being. As a society, we are generally cautious, divided in opinion by race, nervous about the consequences of change, and apprehensive about how we will all get along. We wonder if we will need to sacrifice our cultural identities, traditions, and ethos. Leading our children to their tomorrow while we move through the right-now intensive interactions of competing norms will be a core challenge for many families and educators.

We need strategies for change because, while our primary interest is in Alpha children, we understand profoundly that early interventions without changes in the economic and social landscape for communities will not change their lives as a generation. That is, while public assistance as presently conceived—such as food stamps—may hold an individual family's stress at bay, such interventions may not have transformational effects on generational poverty. On behalf of all Alpha children, we adults need to be as concerned about and as willing to address systemic racism as we are to identify and treat its effects.

In this dynamic national landscape, we use fixed or fluid approaches to change. Simultaneously, there is a growth and deepening of many cultural identities, the empowerment of citizen activists, and widespread access to new communication technologies that are already providing alternative narratives about our national life. Paradoxically, the two groups who are

> "Consult not your fears but your hopes and dreams. Think not about your frustrations, but about your unfulfilled potential. Concern yourself not with what you tried and failed in, but with what is still possible for you to do."[245]
>
> —Pope John XXIII

most disadvantaged economically, African Americans and Latinx, are the most optimistic about the future.

We are all here together at the intersection of new megatrends and, for some, a wistful longing for an era when cultural mythologies could be sustained. At this intersection, all of us must create a new consensus about our national life. Ideologies come and go—but our rainbow children are here and now; they are permanent. To enrich their well-being, we must strive for greater convergence (people coming together to develop commonality) than divergence (people having conflict and profound differences) as we address our technological, economic, and social challenges. It is in this spirit of optimism that, in addition to the aforementioned game changers, three key strategies for both teachers and families will fill the Alpha generation with hope:

- In everything we do, we must consider their futures more than we consider our pasts.

- Actively and intentionally teach our children about diversity and inclusion.

- And, if we must err, err on the side of ensuring our children have intensive relationships with adults and strong social skills.

CONSIDER THE WAY THEY ARE, NOT THE WAY WE WERE

Even in the dimmest light, we see plainly that the childhoods of the Alpha generation are so much different from our own. Still, we are wise to consider how our parenting and teaching are appropriately— or inappropriately—influenced by our own generational experiences. Understanding our own histories can enable us to think about the Alpha children in a more balanced or less judgmental way.

The differences between "them" and "us" can be profound. For example, Alpha children may experience multiple changes in family structures throughout their childhoods that could include an array of step-, half-, and fictive kin as well as interactions with more generations than in the past. The way that Alpha children grow up in constantly evolving families,

> "They will only see their grandparents a handful of times a year. I used to see mine every Sunday night for dinner. Can someone bring me a Kleenex?"[246]
>
> —Sheila Quirke, parent of two young sons

> "Distance is the biggest barrier to seeing grandchildren. Over half of grandparents have at least one grandchild who lives more than 200 miles away, and about a third live more than 50 miles from their closest grandchild."[247]
>
> —AARP 2018 Grandparents Today National Survey

perhaps without the routine presence of grandparents or extended family members, may seem less stable or morally unsound to some of us.

Their tech-immersed worlds require us to have conversations about their media consumption with or without examples from our own lives. As adults, we need to keep up with the proliferation of new social media and apps as our kids move from Snapchat to TikTok to . . . whatever comes next! One father, scaling back his young daughter's time with screens, said: "We also explained that the apps and videos on the iPad were made by some very smart people and were intentionally designed to keep her hooked and habitually watching."[248]

Perhaps we were reared in racially segregated communities, and our children have more multicultural experiences. A mom contrasts her childhood with that of her children: "The folks we saw in the park in 1970s suburbia looked a lot like us—white and from the neighborhood. Now when we hit the park, we see Muslim mothers wearing a variety of burqa, niqab, hijab, or chador. My son thinks they look like cool ninjas. Me, I appreciate the diversity. The Jewish fathers are often wearing dark suits, tzitzits, or kippahs. Little Jewish boys might have payot hanging around their ears or the little Muslim boys might be wearing what look like long dresses to my son. He will hear a variety of languages, too: Spanish, Russian, Hebrew, Polish, Hindi, and on and on and on. I do not exaggerate when I say it is a bit like the United Nations at our park, less than a block from our front door."[249]

Even if our childhoods were amazing, there are many elements of them that are simply not relevant for today's Alpha kids. For example, delaying cell phone use until high school, once a topic of debate, hardly raises concern now. Weekly dressing up for religious service is also passé, as children arrive in the clothing they typically wear daily rather than fancy dresses and miniature suits, if children attend religious services at all. In 2019 the American Enterprise Institute reported significant generational differences in religious upbringing. Younger parents are less likely to participate in religious activities with their children.[250]

Focusing on the way Alpha children are, rather than the way we were, sometimes leads to surprising resistance within ourselves. Refocusing often means that a shift in our head and heart is required. We simply don't want to change. Even change for the better is still change, often initially dreaded and opposed for reasons as human as habits. The status quo seems reasonable, right, compelling, safe.

So, when it comes to our past, we must reevaluate, retain, or relinquish traditions with intentionality—and move forward. For good or ill, we cannot change our past, but our willingness to recognize and confront generational differences can strengthen our relationship with Alpha children. Love is the countervailing force for change and for hope. Love will help us be present with our Alpha children. Then, love will help us anchor on to the future.

Here are some Alpha child characteristics and *responses we might have* as we consider who they are:

- Alpha children and their peers will have normalized a wide variety of family structures. *Welcome each child and family.*

- Alpha children will have an increased focus on equality, openness, transparency, and fairness. *Open up, embrace them, and share our lives.*

- Alpha children are likely to have very diverse educational paths and be in "school" much of their lives. *Change our expectations that our children will follow a predictable educational pathway or that their success depends on any specific pathway.*

- Alpha children will need to learn to work with artificial intelligence and robots. *Help them think about the creativity, adaptability, and technology skills they will need.*

- Alpha children should be prepared to be their own boss at points in their career as a result of technology or the gig economy. *Encourage educational systems to prepare students with specific skills they will need, such as taking initiative, being entrepreneurial, oral and written communication, problem solving, and self-care. Their success will hinge on mastering the four Cs: critical thinking, communication, creativity, and collaboration. Children should start picking up these skills in their early years if they're going to be geared up for the twenty-first century.*

ACTIVELY TEACH YOUR CHILDREN ABOUT DIVERSITY AND INCLUSION

Many parents and teachers of young children believe that topics of race and racial differences should not be discussed with young children, concerned that children might be harmed or upset by these types of conversations. Consequently, teachers who wish to bring these ideas into their learning environments may be hesitant to do so.

Although many people continue to insist that young children do not see race, there is more than fifty years of evidence that clearly demonstrates that children not only see race but that very early in life they understand its social connotations and hierarchies. As Alpha children's first teachers, we are clearly exposing our children to ideas about differences—even our silence teaches them that exploring their questions and expressing their opinions is discouraged.

But filling our children with hope requires us to help them understand the diverse world they inhabit. Staying silent about such a profound reality as their diversity will be unproductive. Because they are already developing impressions and attitudes from us—even if we do nothing! —let's proactively provide them with tools and knowledge they need. The Alpha generation's diversity can very well be its signature strength.

Here are a few ideas of what we adults might do:

- **Alpha children, from their youngest years, already know about race.** Let's educate ourselves and have conversations with our children. Young children exposed to differences gain "fluency" in how to deal with and react to racial differences. Your everyday comments and actions are observed by your children and become a platform for how they learn to respond to human diversity.

- **Alpha children want to learn more about diversity.** Keeping the child's developmental level in mind, talk with children and lay the groundwork for acceptance and respect. Our silence about race makes it taboo. More, do not silence them when they inevitably point out differences (in the grocery store when we find it most embarrassing, for example). Create safe spaces for children to explore questions about what they read or watched. Respond sensitively if your child experienced racial bias themselves.

- **Alpha children learn from visual cues.** Display images of diversity in your home and school that naturally reflect the diversity in the world—books, toys, dolls, games, and other materials.

> "If I do talk about race, will it offend anyone? How do you talk about it in a way that doesn't offend people? . . . I think a lot of teachers will just choose not to address it because if you don't address it, you're not offending anybody. . . . I think this is the problem that we have in our country. . . . We never have an honest, open discussion about race ever."[251]
>
> —*A kindergarten teacher in a racially and economically diverse classroom*

WHAT DO YOUNG CHILDREN KNOW ABOUT RACE?

Today there are increasingly abundant and accessible materials that support children to reject racial bias and embrace diversity. Picture books and multimedia can be found for every age level. Parents and teachers may wish to examine the classic work of Louise Derman-Sparks and her colleagues.[252] What we know about children's development and how they learn about race indicates the critical influence that families and teachers have on idea formation in the first decade of our children's lives:

- **As early as six months**, race-related differences are noticed. As adults, we can present children with images that reflect diversity and offer positive images of their own status.

- **By ages two to four**, children can notice differences among people, and they can also internalize racial bias. Preschoolers begin to notice and point out color, hair, or eye shape differences in the people around you (at the grocery store, at the park, and so forth). Children of this age have learned to classify, and they want to know why! How did these differences occur? Why are two people with different skin tones considered part of the same racial group? As they age, the social connotations of race begin to become clearer (i.e., leading some young Black children to prefer White dolls over Black dolls).[253] As adults, we can respond to their curiosity or concerns with openness and sensitivity.

- **In kindergarten** (ages five and six), as children develop social and cognitive skills and deepen their concepts of fairness, they ask questions about differences, and greater understanding emerges. As adults, we can use children's sense of "righteousness" to introduce concepts of equity.

- **Between five and eleven**, children become clearly aware of racial bias and stereotypes. This awareness can influence their behavior and interactions. For example, test performance decreased for Black and Hispanic children who were aware of stereotypes about their abilities.[254] As adults, we can help children to identify and confront bias, giving voice to their questions and concerns while affirming their individual gifts and collective humanity.

- **By age twelve**, children begin to craft their own beliefs. As adults, we can continually check in with our children and teens to explore their ideas, interpret their experiences, and discuss their interpretations of the media or news events they encounter.

- **Alpha children are watching you!** In order to have thoughtful—and productive—conversations about race with children, we need to be comfortable discussing it ourselves. As adults we support our children when we can both examine our own preconceptions and model the behavior we want to teach. Have, and encourage your children to have, diverse circles of friends. Participate in activities and events from a variety of cultural experiences.

- **Alpha children have a keen sense of justice and fair play.** Studies by Peter Blake and Katherine McAuliffe demonstrate repeatedly that children have a keen sense of what is just and fair, and that these ideals appear to be cross-culturally universal.[255] As work by Louise Derman-Sparks has shown, children can be taught anti-bias strategies, and as adults we can build on their developmental instincts to be kind and compassionate.

- **Alpha children from every background must develop a positive identity.** Derman-Sparks establishes a goal that each child will demonstrate self-awareness, family pride, and a positive sense of social identity. Indeed, culture expresses and perpetuates itself through parenting. Each child should know the value of differences as well as deep, caring human connections. Each child must learn to recognize unfairness and have

> "'You can't be Han Solo . . . you're black.' It hit me out of nowhere. I was so confused. I mean, my skin was certainly darker than anyone else in the group, but since when was that going to stop the game about space aliens? I assumed they sensed my confusion and offered me the role as Lando instead, because 'He looked more like you.' It was the day that my mother explained racism to me."[256]
>
> —*Nathaniel K. Jones, MD, writing about racism for the American Academy of Pediatrics Voices blog*

language to describe it, along with the sense of how much it hurts. And each child can develop the skills to act with others or alone against prejudice and biased actions.

Having challenging conversations with our Alpha children conveys important information to them, builds their sense that we are a trusted source of information, and most important, establishes strong bonds with them. Yes, as teachers and parents we are unmistakable agents of socialization. But our children also teach us as they develop their own understandings, process their personal experiences, and engage in intricate patterns of mutual interactions with us throughout their lives.

ENSURE OUR CHILDREN HAVE INTENSIVE RELATIONSHIPS WITH ADULTS AND STRONG SOCIAL SKILLS

Reports describe Generation Alpha as one that will be super smart, entrepreneurial, and inventive. So, we families and teachers really need to be super smart and insightful, too, as we consider anew the twenty-first century skills that Generation Alpha needs. And therein lies the rub. By the time the oldest of them graduates high school in 2030, "the way we were" as parents and educators may be less relevant to children who learned more from screens than from books.

But radical change will arrive long before then, and our children's experiences may amaze us. Already, as a generation, many of them attend child care centers and preschools that are polyglot mosaics representing a vast spectrum of races, religions, languages, families, and cultures. These members of the class of 2030 are hardwired to see technology as a major source of both education and entertainment, and in tandem we can anticipate that automation will continually and rapidly advance in the lives of Alpha children.

> "Everybody growing up needs somebody who says, 'I believe in you, you're OK, things are going to be all right.'"[257]
>
> —Oprah Winfrey

The adults in their lives must understand and prepare them: as "robots" advance, the most prized skills will be very "human" ones. In essence, we must be sure that our children are developing strong social and collaboration skills. And we must recognize that our Alpha generation cohort may need extra help when it comes to the human connections and soft skills that computers aren't good at: interpersonal communication and creativity, problem solving, and relationship building. We must tend to their holistic development. We must be sure that they have strong relationships with the adults in their lives, not just their screens.

There have been many debates about whether early childhood education, especially in the prekindergarten years, should focus on the social and emotional development of children in contrast to "skills-specific curricula," namely numeracy and literacy. For Alpha children, the answer is not either/or. Teaching that is based on play and social-emotional skills is mutually complementary to more academic instruction. Both benefit kids' readiness for school. Indeed, research suggests that teachers who do a better job of cultivating emotional skills and work ethic in their students are more likely to see their students succeed than teachers who simply raise test scores.

Relationships matter in virtually all ways that promote positive child development. A

> "Nothing will ever take the place of one person actually being with another person. . . . There can be lots of fancy things like TV and radio and telephones and internet, but nothing can take the place of people interacting face to face."[258]
>
> "No matter how helpful computers are as tools, and, of course, they can be very helpful tools, they don't begin to compare in significance to the teacher-child relationship, which is human and mutual. A computer can help you learn to spell HUG, but it can never know the risk or the joy of actually giving or receiving one."[259]
>
> —*Fred Rogers, children's television personality*

nurturing, familiar, stable, and responsive relationship with adults—especially primary caregivers—is essential to optimize child development and social relationships. Playing with children encourages them to explore, observe, experiment, and solve problems. Children's experiences with their parents within a cultural context consequently scaffold them to become culturally competent members of their society.

In the early years there are two areas of social-emotional competence that must be highlighted: the family's role in boosting brain development and the critical importance of positive teacher-child interactions.

Area 1: Boost baby's brains. As neuroscience is maturing, researchers have uncovered an astounding rate of brain development in babies and toddlers. Continuous and predictable interactions with the adults in their lives play a critical role in this development. As pediatrician T. Berry Brazelton points out, brain development is a lifelong project—but the impact of the early years is profound due to the brain's plasticity at that time.

> "Attachment to a baby is a long-term process, not a single, magical moment. The opportunity for bonding at birth may be compared to falling in love—staying in love takes longer and demands more work."
>
> —T. Berry Brazelton[260]

Many resources exist to support the baby's emergent language, thinking, and emotional skills.[261] A major idea is that reciprocal interactions with children—dubbed "serve and return" interactions—are a platform for their intellectual stimulation. For example, if a baby coos, the mom smiles back. These conversations respect babies as communication partners long before infants produce language. Continuous responsive interactions with people form and strengthen synapses or connections in the child's brain. Further, these interactions model the social relationships that will shape children's future contacts with others throughout their lives.

While strong relationships are critical for all Alpha children, they are particularly important for children who live in challenging environments.

Reflecting different environments, the frontal and parietal lobes of the brains of children in poverty have much less grey matter than the brains of children who are not poor. Though newborns across income groups have the same amount of grey matter in their brains, differences show up in the first three years of life, and this affects their school readiness even before they enter kindergarten classrooms. The differences also affect children's social skills and may result in behavioral problems as well as academic challenges. An exceptionally supportive environment is perhaps the best intervention for helping these children succeed in school and beyond, according to the Robert Woods Johnson Foundation.[262]

Area 2: Early childhood educators must focus on positive interactions and brain building too. Many Alpha children will be spending much of their time with early childhood educators in environments that must also ensure responsive, warm, and supportive interactions with them. These interactions build the foundation for learning. The best quality early childhood programs are characterized by a high level of intentionality from teachers, who continuously acknowledge children's individual differences. All interactions and conversations that an educator

CHANGING PHILOSOPHIES

Thoughts about our interactions and relationships with children have changed over time. What seemed normal in one era might appear bizarre, even psychologically damaging, in another:

"Never hug and kiss them or let them sit on your lap. . . . Shake hands with them in the morning. Give them a pat on the head if they have made an extraordinarily good job of a difficult task. If you must, kiss them once on the forehead when they say goodnight."[263]

—Behaviorist John Watson, Psychological Care of the Infant and Child, *1928*

has with children can influence how children learn, grow, and feel about themselves.

Generation Alpha must cultivate soft skills such as regulating their own behavior, responding to the behavior of others, and growing positive dispositions for learning. Current research stresses the importance of strong teacher-child interactions in producing these outcomes. There is also renewed emphasis on critical thinking and creative problem solving, particularly through collaborative efforts in which children set goals and demonstrate how they achieved them. With these interactions, teachers acknowledge and are responsive to individual differences, offer sensitive caregiving, engage in reciprocal talk that enhances language development, foster engagement, and stimulate the child's thinking. It's a big job!

> "It takes more than love of teaching for a person to be an effective early educator. However, it became very rewarding when I became more intentional in the teaching strategies I used and saw the difference it made in the development of my pupils. Developing foundational skills in young children is a complex job that requires competency and skill. Those who work with the youngest children must know how to build trust with children and families."[264]
>
> —Michele Miller-Cox, an infant-toddler teacher in Cary, North Carolina

THE WAY FORWARD

Offering more support to families and teachers, enabling them to perform their important roles, is a major opportunity for our nation. That's why we emphasize the game changers of new types of family support, enhanced early childhood education, and opportunity equity for the Alpha generation. As millions of young children spend a large part of their childhood with early childhood educators, it is imperative that we offer them greater respect for their competence, acknowledge their strengths, and ensure equity for them.

The way forward requires change—a paradigm shift. Applying Thomas Kuhn's ideas to Generation Alpha, we expect that, when these breakthroughs occur and the game changers are accepted, they will lead to large, impressive changes. We expect that people will behave differently, but even more important, actually see their world from a new perspective. These game changers would therefore represent a bifurcation point—a fork in the road that opens up a completely new way of perceiving, thinking, and taking action, with no turning back. Once the paradigm threshold is crossed, we will never again see our way of life the same as we do now.

For many of us, hope for paradigm-shifting change seems like a reasonable forecast. The greater risk is that we do nothing, that cynicism stifles our imaginations, that we move so slowly in the face of strong evidence that our opportunities for transformation are stilted. Hope, with action, is the better alternative when the stakes are so high.

The stakes are higher because the megatrends are inevitable. So we must think differently. We must act differently in roles we perform almost instinctively. As families and teachers, we are powerful agents of cultural transmission. Most of this transmission occurs beneath our consciousness and comes forth as "the way we do things" in our families and communities. The Alpha generation poses an opportunity for us to bring more consciousness to our roles. With an abundance of hope, parents and the early childhood workforce must think carefully about how we can meet the needs of these contemporary children.

It is not easy to be a parent. It is not easy to be a teacher. Both teachers and parents often have fewer resources, and more pressure, than they need. For adults, this pressure can induce stress. We place high value on good parenting and effective teaching as extremely important to our identities and our children's identities. We all recognize the need for more institutional support in our journeys—thus our clarion call for significant game changers.

HOPE FOR EARLY CHILDHOOD EDUCATORS

The hope we bring to the Alpha generation is also extended to early childhood educators. In *Guiding Principles for the New Early Childhood Educator*, my colleague Brenda Gadson and I identify four key tenets for progress. Early childhood educators need and must have more of the following:

- **Respect:** Society at large must acknowledge and demonstrate absolute dignity for practitioners. Professionalizing the field should focus on professional capital rather than individual worker shortcomings. We cannot keep asking educators to simply wait for changes such as comparable compensation for their roles as educators.

- **Recognition of their competence:** Early childhood educators must more clearly define and articulate to the public the observable, measurable, and distinct contributions to child and family life.

- **Preservation of perennial strengths:** One of the most critical responsibilities of leadership is deciding what must *not* change during eras of change. What are the cross-generational strengths or fundamental assets of child development that are essential for families or educators to retain and bring forward? For example, as technology use increases, soft skills such as interpersonal communication may matter more than ever.

- **Equity:** Our educational systems must address the pervasive disparities experienced by early childhood educators. This will require more equitable investments in children under age five, relative to the public support directed to older children. Enhancing support to both early childhood educators and the children they serve are education as well as social justice issues.[265]

We hope because, in true American spirit, we believe that the future is unwritten. Megatrends simply show the way away from the contemporary systems which, as it turns out, aren't very modern at all.

We can help Generation Alpha be prepared to confront the big challenges of their time. True, there is no one right way to parent or to teach. There is no script. But with our focus on building relationships and soft skills, I believe—hope—we will well support our children's futures and opportunities for who they are going to be.

As this book is being completed, our nation is in the midst of a coronavirus pandemic, a worldwide disruption in our economic systems and personal lives. What seemed impossible months ago—extensive telework, for example—has become routine and widely accepted. What seemed normal in the first months of 2020—gatherings in theaters, churches, parks, and restaurants—are right now an anomaly. But through the stunning developments we witness an outpouring of compassion, new forms of fellowship, redistribution of resources, and expanded capacity to see the world through the perspectives of others. We more clearly recognize our interdependence, and our sense of unity is sharpened. For many of our eldest Alpha children, this will be a defining memory of their lives.

But children do not live in the long term; their childhoods are NOW. And the choices we make today have a large role in determining the outcomes we will witness tomorrow.

Today we play with them, we answer their questions, we listen, we learn. Together, as families and educators, we raise and teach our Alpha kids.

The journey ahead of us is clear. There are four essentials we must take with us on the journey as we walk alongside the Alpha generation:

- **A big dose of *courage*:** Because when it matters most, we have always been strong in the face of radical disruptions. We must call upon our courage—activate our *cour* (love)—and realize that challenges can be overcome.

- **Unparalleled *confidence*:** Because when we decide to make a difference, we always have. Confidence is believing that our families are worthy of greater support and our educators worthy of more respect. These paradigm shifts are just.

- **Unwavering *commitment*:** Because we are a people who get things done once we make up our minds to do so. As Yoda said, "Do. Or do not. There is no try." Commitments are powerful pledges we make to ourselves to carry out a course of action. Commitment brings hope to life.

- ***Imagination*:** If we cannot imagine it, we cannot create it. And the only way to create something new is by first imagining it. Our imagination is driven by and reflects our innermost values and beliefs. It encourages us to believe in more than we know.

I am encouraged by the success we will achieve on this journey. Be hopeful! I have great faith that we will do the right thing for the Alpha generation. As President Franklin D. Roosevelt once said, "We may not be able to prepare the future for our children, but we can at least prepare our children for the future."[266] So, let's be game changers!

NOTES

CHAPTER ONE

1. *Global Trends 2030: Alternative Worlds* (Washington, DC: National Intelligence Council, 2012), www.dni.gov/files/documents/GlobalTrends_2030.pdf.

2. Dennis Gabor, *Inventing the Future* (New York: Alfred A. Knopf, 1963), 207.

3. Daisaku Ikeda, *Hope Is a Decision* (Santa Monica, CA: Middleway Press, 2017).

4. "Population Estimates Show Aging Across Race Groups Differs," United States Census Bureau, June 20, 2019, www.census.gov/newsroom/press-releases/2019/estimates-characteristics.html.

5. "An Aging Nation: Projected Number of Children and Older Adults," United States Census Bureau, October 8, 2019, www.census.gov/library/visualizations/2018/comm/historic-first.html.

6. Kim Parker, Rich Morin, and Juliana Menasce Horowitz, "Looking to the Future, Public Sees an America in Decline on Many Fronts," Pew Research Center, March 21, 2019, https://www.pewsocialtrends.org/2019/03/21/public-sees-an-america-in-decline-on-many-fronts.

7. Timothy B. Lee, "New Research Suggests an Aging Workforce Is Holding Back Economic Growth," *Vox*, September 26, 2016, www.vox.com/a/new-economy-future/aging-population-slow-growth.

8. William H. Frey, "Less Than Half of US Children Under 15 Are White, Census Shows," The Brookings Institution, June 24, 2019, www.brookings.edu/research/less-than-half-of-us-children-under-15-are-White-census-shows.

9. William O'Hare, "The Changing Child Population of the United States: Analysis of Data from the 2010 Census" (working paper, The Annie E. Casey Foundation, 2011), 1. https://files.eric.ed.gov/fulltext/ED527048.pdf.

10. Sandra L. Colby and Jennifer M. Ortman, *Projections of the Size and Composition of the U.S. Population: 2014 to 2060* (Washington, DC: Census Bureau, March 2015), 9. www.census.gov/content/dam/Census/library/publications/2015/demo/p25-1143.pdf.

11. William H. Frey, "Less Than Half of US Children Under 15 Are White, Census Shows," The Brookings Institution, June 24, 2019, www.brookings.edu/research/less-than-half-of-us-children-under-15-are-White-census-shows.

12. "Older People Projected to Outnumber Children for First Time in U.S. History," United States Census Bureau, revised October 8, 2019, www.census.gov/newsroom/press-releases/2018/cb18-41-population-projections.html.

13. Kendra Yoshinaga, "Babies of Color Are Now the Majority, Census Says," National Public Radio, July 1, 2016, www.npr.org/sections/ed/2016/07/01/484325664/babies-of-color-are-now-the-majority-census-says.

14. Rogelio Sáenz and Kenneth Johnson, *White Deaths Exceed Births in a Majority of U.S. States* (Madison, WI: Applied Population Lab, 2018), https://apl.wisc.edu/briefs_resources/pdf/natural-decrease-18.pdf.

15. "America's Children: Key National Indicators of Well-Being, 2019," Childstats, United States Department of Education, www.childstats.gov/americaschildren/demo.asp.

16. William H. Frey, "The US Will Become 'Minority White' in 2045, Census Projects: Youthful Minorities Are the Engine of Future Growth," Brookings Institution, March 14, 2018, www.brookings.edu/blog/the-avenue/2018/03/14/the-us-will-become-minority-white-in-2045-census-projects/; William H. Frey, "Diversity Explosion: How New Racial Demographics Are Remaking America," Brookings Institution, July 24, 2018, www.brookings.edu/book/diversity-explosion-2.

17. William H. Frey, "The US Will Become 'Minority White' in 2045, Census Projects: Youthful Minorities Are the Engine of Future Growth," Brookings Institution, March 14, 2018, www.brookings.edu/blog/the-avenue/2018/03/14/the-us-will-become-minority-white-in-2045-census-projects.

18. Rogelio Sáenz and Dudley L. Poston Jr, "Children of Color Already Make Up the Majority of Kids in Many US States," The Conversation, January 9, 2020, https://theconversation.com/children-of-color-already-make-up-the-majority-of-kids-in-many-us-states-128499.

19. Leila Morsy and Richard Rothstein, *Mass Incarceration and Children's Outcomes: Criminal Justice Policy Is Education Policy* (Washington, DC: Economic Policy Institute, 2016), www.epi.org/files/pdf/118615.pdf.

20. Valerie Wilson and Jessica Scheider, "The Rise in Children Poverty Reveals Racial Inequality, More Than a Failed War on Poverty," Economic Policy Institute, June 8, 2018, https://www.epi.org/publication/the-rise-in-child-poverty-reveals-racial-inequality-more-than-a-failed-war-on-poverty.

21. *Race for Results* (Baltimore: Annie E. Casey Foundation, 2017), www.aecf.org/m/resourcedoc/aecf-2017raceforresults-2017.pdf.

22. Patrick B. McGrady and John R. Reynolds, "Racial Mismatch in the Classroom: Beyond Black-White Differences," *Sociology of Education* 86, no. 1 (2013): 3–17, https://journals.sagepub.com/doi/full/10.1177/0038040712444857.

23. Lynda Laughlin, *Who's Minding the Kids? Child Care Arrangements: Spring 2011* (Washington, DC: United States Census Bureau, April 2013), https://www.census.gov/prod/2013pubs/p70-135.pdf; "How Do We Know? Child Care an Important Part of American Life," United States Census Bureau, June 2013, www.census.gov/library/visualizations/2013/comm/child_care.html.

24. Robin DiAngelo, *White Fragility: Why It's So Hard for White People to Talk about Racism* (Boston: Beacon Press, 2018), 14.

25. Valora Washington and Lisa Yarkony, *Child Care for All: Finding the Will and the Way* (Washington, DC: Council for Professional Recognition, 2019), www.cdacouncil.org/newsletter/1288-child-care-for-all-finding-the-will-and-the-way.

26. Valora Washington and Lisa Yarkony, *Child Care for All: Finding the Will and the Way* (Washington, DC: Council for Professional Recognition, 2019), www.cdacouncil.org/newsletter/1288-child-care-for-all-finding-the-will-and-the-way.

27. Caitlin McLean, Marcy Whitebook, and Eunice Roh, *From Unlivable Wages to Just Pay for Early Educators* (Berkeley: Center for the Study of Child Care Employment, University of California, Berkeley, 2019), https://cscce.berkeley.edu/files/2019/05/From-Unlivable-Wages-to-Just-Pay-for-Early-Educators.pdf.

28. Valora Washington and Lisa Yarkony, *Child Care for All: Finding the Will and the Way* (Washington, DC: Council for Professional Recognition, 2019), www.cdacouncil.org/newsletter/1288-child-care-for-all-finding-the-will-and-the-way.

29. William T. Dickens, Isabel Sawhill, and Jeffrey Tebbs, *The Effects of Investing in Early Education on Economic Growth* (Washington, DC: The Brookings Institution, April 2006), www.brookings.edu/wp-content/uploads/2016/06/pb153.pdf.

30. Rhian Evans Allvin, "Making Connections. Early Childhood Educators and the American Economy: An American Story," *Young Children* 72, no. 5 (November 2017), www.naeyc.org/resources/pubs/yc/nov2017/making-connections.

31. P. Pizzo et al., "The Ripple Effect: California Early Care and Education Contributes at Least $24.5 Billion Annually to Economic Output in the State," LinkedIn, May 7, 2020, www.linkedin.com/pulse/ripple-effect-california-early-care-education-least-245-pizzo/?trk=portfolio_article-card_title&fbclid=IwAR2oAX49eQgiU30LbkLcejiKk2L5Okg NI1-j8z7HFc_SXrWdy_wmqNZa-wE.

32. Robin DiAngelo, *White Fragility: Why It's So Hard for White People to Talk about Racism* (Boston: Beacon Press, 2018).

33. Courtney Martin, "Why Are White People So Bad at Talking about Race?" Brightthemag.com, September 7, 2018, https://brightthemag.com/White-fragility-why-are-White-people-so-bad-at-talking-about-race-robin-diangelo-White-privilege-dbd5b92ba210.

34. Barack Obama, "Barack Obama's New Hampshire Primary Speech," *New York Times*, January 8, 2008, www.nytimes.com/2008/01/08/us/politics/08text-obama.html

CHAPTER TWO

35. Reis Thebault, Andrew Ba Tran, and Vanessa Williams, "The Coronavirus Is Infecting and Killing Black Americans at an Alarmingly High Rate," *Washington Post*, April 7, 2020, www.washingtonpost.com/nation/2020/04/07/coronavirus-is-infecting-killing-black-americans-an-alarmingly-high-rate-post-analysis-shows/?arc404=true.

36. *World Population Prospects 2019: Highlights* (United Nations, Department of Economic and Social Affairs, Population Division, 2019), 1, https://population.un.org/wpp/Publications/Files/WPP2019_Highlights.pdf.

37. Christine Michel Carter, "The Complete Guide to Generation Alpha, the Children of Millennials," *Forbes*, December 21, 2016, www.forbes.com/sites/christinecarter/2016/12/21/the-complete-guide-to-generation-alpha-the-children-of-millennials/#4e37a3393623.

38. Nicole Lyn Pesce, "U.S. Life Expectancy Rises for the First Time in Four Years—Here's How Much Longer Americans Are Living," MarketWatch, January 31, 2020, www.marketwatch.com/story/americans-are-living-a-month-longer-as-us-life-expectancy-rises-for-the-first-time-in-four-years-2020-01-30.

39. Sarah H. Matthews and Rongjun Sun, "Incidence of Four-Generation Family Lineages: Is Timing of Fertility or Mortality a Better Explanation?" *The Journals of Gerontology: Series B* 61, no. 2 (March 1, 2006): S99–S106, https://doi.org/10.1093/geronb/61.2.S99.

40. Emily M. Agree, "Demography of Aging and the Family," In *Future Directions for the Demography of Aging: Proceedings of a Workshop*, eds. M. K. Majmundar and M. D. Hayward, (Bethesda, MD: National Center for Biotechnology Information, U.S. National Library of Medicine National Academies Press, 2018), www.ncbi.nlm.nih.gov/books/NBK513078.

41. Bruce Cannon Gibney, *A Generation of Sociopaths: How the Baby Boomers Betrayed America* (New York: Hachette Books, 2017), 348.

42. Ben Schiller, "Baby Boomers Stole the American Dream, But Young People Can Take It Back," Fastcompany.com, March 22, 2018, www.fastcompany.com/40545713/baby-boomers-stole-the-american-dream-but-young-people-can-take-it-back.

43. Erin Duffin, "Average Number of Own Children Under 18 in Families with Children in the United States from 1960 to 2019," Statista.com, January 13, 2020, www.statista.com/statistics/718084/average-number-of-own-children-per-family.

44. George Gao, "Americans' Ideal Family Size Is Smaller Than It Used to Be," Pew Research Center, May 8, 2015, www.pewresearch.org/fact-tank/2015/05/08/ideal-size-of-the-american-family.

45. Julia B. Isaacs, Isabel V. Sawhill, and Ron Haskins, *Getting Ahead or Losing Ground: Economic Mobility in America* (Washington, DC: The Brookings Institution, 2016), www.brookings.edu/wp-content/uploads/2016/06/02_economic_mobility_sawhill.pdf.

46. George Gao, "Americans' Ideal Family Size Is Smaller Than It Used to Be," Pew Research Center, May 8, 2015, www.pewresearch.org/fact-tank/2015/05/08/ideal-size-of-the-american-family.

47. George Gao, "Americans' Ideal Family Size Is Smaller Than It Used to Be," Pew Research Center, May 8, 2015, www.pewresearch.org/fact-tank/2015/05/08/ideal-size-of-the-american-family.

48. United States Department of Agriculture, "Expenditures on Children by Families Reports—All Years," 2017, www.fns.usda.gov/resource/expenditures-children-families-reports-all-years.

49. Mark Lino, "The Cost of Raising a Child," United States Department of Agriculture, February 18, 2020, www.usda.gov/media/blog/2017/01/13/cost-raising-child.

50. "Number of Children," Child Trends, 2019, https://www.childtrends.org/indicators/number-of-children.

51. "1. The American Family Today," Pew Research Center, December 17, 2015, www.pewsocialtrends.org/2015/12/17/1-the-american-family-today.

52. "Parenting in America: Outlook, Worries, Aspirations Are Strongly Linked to Financial Situation," Pew Research Center, December 17, 2015, www.pewsocialtrends.org/wp-content/uploads/sites/3/2015/12/2015-12-17_parenting-in-america_FINAL.pdf.

53. Gretchen Livingston, "The Rise of Single Fathers: A Ninefold Increase Since 1960," Pew Research Center, July 2, 2013, www.pewsocialtrends.org/2013/07/02/the-rise-of-single-fathers.

54. "1. The American Family Today," Pew Research Center, December 17, 2015, www.pewsocialtrends.org/2015/12/17/1-the-american-family-today.

55. "1. The American Family Today," Pew Research Center, December 17, 2015, www.pewsocialtrends.org/2015/12/17/1-the-american-family-today.

56. Melissa Schneider, "Study: How Millennial Parents Are Preparing Their Kids for a Life Online," GoDaddy.com, August 23, 2018, www.godaddy.com/garage/study-how-millennial-parents-are-preparing-their-kids-for-a-life-online.

57. Kellie Scott, "Instagram Accounts for Babies Are Becoming More Popular. This Is What Parents Should Consider," ABC Life, October 10, 2019, www.abc.net.au/life/considerations-starting-a-social-media-account-for-your-child/11524188.

58. Patrick Wright, "Should Children Decide What Photos of Them Are Shared Online? Here's What You Had to Say," ABC Life, February 25, 2019, www.abc.net.au/life/sharing-photos-of-children-online-parents-respond/10837448.

59. "What Impact Will Artificial Intelligence Have on the Lives of 'Generation Alpha'? A Study of Millennial Parents of Generation Alpha Kids," Institute of Electrical and Electronics Engineers, June 13–15, 2017, https://transmitter.ieee.org/wp-content/uploads/2017/06/Gen-AI-Infographic-V2.6.pdf.

60. Christopher Munsey, "Bring Back Old-Fashioned Play," *Monitor on Psychology* 39, no. 9 (2008): 52, www.apa.org/monitor/2008/10/play.

61. "Parenting in America: Outlook, Worries, Aspirations Are Strongly Linked to Financial Situation," Pew Research Center, December 17, 2015, www.pewsocialtrends.org/2015/12/17/parenting-in-america.

62. Council on Communications and Media, "Media and Young Minds," *American Academy of Pediatrics* 138, no. 5 (November 1, 2016): 1–8, https://pediatrics.aappublications.org/content/pediatrics/138/5/e20162591.full.pdf.

63. Padma Ravichandran, Brandel France De Bravo, and Rebecca Beauport, "Young Children and Screen Time (TV, Computers, Etc.)," National Center for Health Research, www.center4research.org/young-children-screen-time-tv-computers-etc, accessed July 22, 2020.

64. Genevieve Shaw Brown, "After Gen Z, Meet Gen Alpha. What to Know about the Generation Born 2010 to Today," *Good Morning America*, February 17, 2020, www.goodmorningamerica.com/family/story/gen-meet-gen-alpha-generation-born-2010-today-68971965.

65. Diana Bradley, "'I Would Prefer an iPad to a Dog': Generation Alpha Talks Technology in Hotwire Video," *PR Week*, September 25, 2018, www.prweek.com/article/1493880/i-prefer-ipad-dog-generation-alpha-talks-technology-hotwire-video.

66. Christine Michel Carter, "The Complete Guide to Generation Alpha, the Children of Millennials," *Forbes*, December 21, 2016, www.forbes.com/sites/christinecarter/2016/12/21/the-complete-guide-to-generation-alpha-the-children-of-millennials/#34465f2b3623.

67. Somini Sengupta, "The World Has a Problem: Too Many Young People," *New York Times*, March 5, 2016, www.nytimes.com/2016/03/06/sunday-review/the-world-has-a-problem-too-many-young-people.html.

68. Hannah Hartig and Hannah Gilberstadt, "Younger Americans More Likely Than Older Adults to Say There Are Other Countries That Are Better Than the U.S." Pew Research Center, January 8, 2020, www.pewresearch.org/fact-tank/2020/01/08/younger-americans-more-likely-than-older-adults-to-say-there-are-other-countries-that-are-better-than-the-u-s.

69. "Most Americans Say State Governments Have Lifted COVID-19 Restrictions Too Quickly," Pew Research Center, August 6, 2020, www.pewresearch.org/politics/2020/08/06/most-americans-say-state-governments-have-lifted-covid-19-restrictions-too-quickly.

70. Ian Tyrrell, "What, Exactly, Is 'American Exceptionalism'?," The Week, October 21, 2016, https://theweek.com/articles/654508/what-exactly-american-exceptionalism.

71. Yuval Noah Harari, *21 Lessons for the 21st Century* (New York: Spiegel & Grau, 2018).

72. William H. Frey, "Less Than Half of US Children Under 15 Are White, Census Shows: Declines in White Youth Population Are Countered by Gains in Other Racial Groups," The Brookings Institution, July 17, 2019, www.brookings.edu/research/less-than-half-of-us-children-under-15-are-white-census-shows.

73. "Racial and Ethnic Composition of the Child Population," Child Trends, December 13, 2018, www.childtrends.org/indicators/racial-and-ethnic-composition-of-the-child-population.

74. "Chapter 2: Immigration's Impact on Past and Future U.S. Population Change," Pew Research Center, September 28, 2015, www.pewresearch.org/hispanic/2015/09/28/chapter-2-immigrations-impact-on-past-and-future-u-s-population-change.

75. William H. Frey, "Less Than Half of US Children Under 15 Are White, Census Shows: Declines in White Youth Population Are Countered by Gains in Other Racial Groups," The Brookings Institution, July 17, 2019, www.brookings.edu/research/less-than-half-of-us-children-under-15-are-white-census-shows.

76. "Chapter 2: Immigration's Impact on Past and Future U.S. Population Change," Pew Research Center, September 28, 2015, www.pewresearch.org/hispanic/2015/09/28/chapter-2-immigrations-impact-on-past-and-future-u-s-population-change.

77. William H. Frey, "Less Than Half of US Children Under 15 Are White, Census Shows: Declines in White Youth Population Are Countered by Gains in Other Racial Groups," The Brookings Institution, July 17, 2019, www.brookings.edu/research/less-than-half-of-us-children-under-15-are-white-census-shows.

78. "Chapter 2: Immigration's Impact on Past and Future U.S. Population Change," Pew Research Center, September 28, 2015, www.pewresearch.org/hispanic/2015/09/28/chapter-2-immigrations-impact-on-past-and-future-u-s-population-change.

79. William H. Frey, "Less Than Half of US Children Under 15 Are White, Census Shows: Declines in White Youth Population Are Countered by Gains in Other Racial Groups," The Brookings Institution, July 17, 2019, www.brookings.edu/research/less-than-half-of-us-children-under-15-are-white-census-shows.

80. Anthony Daniel Perez and Charles Hirschman, "The Changing Racial and Ethnic Composition of the US Population: Emerging American Identities," *Population and Development Review* 35, no. 1 (March 2009): 1–51, www.ncbi.nlm.nih.gov/pmc/articles/PMC2882688/pdf/nihms-102416.pdf.

81. Luke Stangel, "Are You Ready for the Talent Crunch? How Workforce Development Programs Turn Talent Puddles into Talent Pools," Graduate School of Stanford Business, February 22, 2017, www.gsb.stanford.edu/insights/are-you-ready-talent-crunch.

82. Elaine Pofeldt, "Freelancers Now Make Up 35% of U.S. Workforce," *Forbes*, October 6, 2016, www.forbes.com /sites/elainepofeldt/2016/10/06/new-survey-freelance-economy-shows-rapid-growth/#30a32b257c3f; Shane McFeely, and Ryan Pendell, "What Workplace Leaders Can Learn from the Real Gig Economy," Gallup, August 16, 2018, www.gallup.com/workplace/240929/workplace-leaders-learn-real-gig-economy.aspx.

83. Yuval Noah Harari, *21 Lessons for the 21st Century* (New York: Spiegel & Grau, 2018), 37.

84. Yuval Noah Harari, *21 Lessons for the 21st Century* (New York: Spiegel & Grau, 2018), 36.

85. Yuval Noah Harari, *21 Lessons for the 21st Century* (New York: Spiegel & Grau, 2018), 72.

CHAPTER THREE

86. "Parenting in America: Outlook, Worries, Aspirations Are Strongly Linked to Financial Situation," Pew Research Center, December 17, 2015, www.pewsocialtrends.org/2015/12/17/parenting-in-america.

87. "Children in Nature: Improving Health by Reconnecting Youth with the Outdoors," Ashburn, VA: National Recreation and Park Association, www.nrpa.org/uploadedFiles/nrpa.org/Advocacy/Children-in-Nature.pdf.

88. "Parenting in America: Outlook, Worries, Aspirations Are Strongly Linked to Financial Situation," Pew Research Center, December 17, 2015, www.pewsocialtrends.org/2015/12/17/parenting-in-america.

89. "Parenting in America: Outlook, Worries, Aspirations Are Strongly Linked to Financial Situation," Pew Research Center, December 17, 2015, www.pewsocialtrends.org/2015/12/17/parenting-in-america.

CHAPTER FOUR

90. Ta-Nehisi Coates, "The Case for Reparations," *The Atlantic*, June 2014, www.theatlantic.com/magazine /archive/2014/06/the-case-for-reparations/361631.

91. James Traslow Adams, *The Epic of America* (New Brunswick, NJ: Transaction Publishers, 2012), https://books. google.com/books/about/The_Epic_of_America.html?id=paIpt-vBVR8C.

92. Michael Young, *The Rise of the Meritocracy* (London: Routledge, 1958), https://books.google.com/ books?id=QelNAQAAQBAJ&printsec=frontcover&source=gbs_ge_summary_r&cad=0#v=onepage&q&f=false.

93. Frederick Douglass, *Self-Made Men* (Bennington, NH: Monadnock Valley Press, 1872), http://monadnock.net/ douglass/self-made-men.html.

94. Jennifer Glass, Robin W. Simon, and Matthew A. Andersson, "Parenthood and Happiness: Effects of Work-Family Reconciliation Policies in 22 OECD Countries," *American Journal of Sociology* 122, no. 3 (November 2016): 886–929. https://epc2014.princeton.edu/papers/140098
KJ Dell'Antonia, "For U.S. Parents, a Troubling Happiness Gap," *New York Times*, June 17, 2016, https:// well.blogs.nytimes.com/2016/06/17/for-u-s-parents-a-troubling-happiness-gap.

95. Jennifer Glass, "Parenting and Happiness in 22 Countries," Council on Contemporary Families, June 15, 2016, https://contemporaryfamilies.org/brief-parenting-happiness.

96. "The Global Social Mobility Report 2020: Equality, Opportunity and a New Economic Imperative," World Economic Forum, January 2020, www3.weforum.org/docs/Global_Social_Mobility_Report.pdf.

97. Hanna Ziady, "The American Dream Is Much Easier to Achieve in Canada, Report Finds," CTV News, January 20, 2020, www.ctvnews.ca/world/the-american-dream-is-much-easier-to -achieve-in-canada-report-finds-1.4775201.

98. Heather C. Hill, "50 Years Ago, One Report Introduced Americans to the Black-White Achievement Gap. Here's What We've Learned Since," Chalkbeat, July 13, 2016, https://chalkbeat.org/posts/us/2016/07/13/50-years-ago- the-coleman-report-revealed-the-black-white-achievement-gap-in-america-heres-what-weve-learned-since.

99. Julia B. Isaacs, Isabel V. Sawhill, and Ron Haskins, *Getting Ahead or Losing Ground: Economic Mobility in America* (Washington, DC: The Brookings Institution, 2016), www.brookings.edu/wp-content/uploads/2016/06 /02_economic_mobility_sawhill.pdf.

100. Raj Chetty, John Friedman, Emmanuel Saez, Nicholas Turner, and Danny Yagan, "Income Segregation and Intergenerational Mobility Across Colleges in the United States," *Opportunity Insights,* February 2020, https:// opportunityinsights.org/paper/undermatching/; Richard V. Reeves, and Eleanor Krause, "Raj Chetty in 14 Charts: Big Findings on Opportunity and Mobility We Should All Know," The Brookings Institution, January 11, 2018, www.brookings.edu/blog/social-mobility-memos/2018/01/11/raj-chetty-in-14-charts-big -findings-on-opportunity-and-mobility-we-should-know.

101. Kyle Kowalski, "Is the American Dream Waking Up? The Truth about Social Mobility in the US," Sloww.co, www.sloww.co/american-dream-mobility/, accessed July 25, 2020; Julia B. Isaacs, "International Comparisons of Economic Mobility," in *Getting Ahead or Losing Ground*, by Julia B. Isaacs, Isabel V. Sawhill, and Ron Haskins,

(Washington, DC: The Brookings Institution, 2016), 37–46. https://www.brookings.edu/wp-content /uploads/2016/06/02_economic_mobility_sawhill.pdf.

102. Alia E. Dastagir, "Why American Moms Are Seriously Struggling," *USA Today*, May 9, 2019, https://www. usatoday.com/in-depth/news/nation/2019/05/09/working-moms-motherhood-stress-parenting-good-mom-childcare-daycare-costs-maternity-leave-gender-gap/3586366002.

103. KJ Dell'Antonia, "For U.S. Parents, a Troubling Happiness Gap," *New York Times*, June 17, 2016, https://well. blogs.nytimes.com/2016/06/17/for-u-s-parents-a-troubling-happiness-gap.

104. Sean Fleming, "These Countries Have the Most Expensive Childcare," World Economic Forum, April 23, 2019, www.weforum.org/agenda/2019/04/these-countries-have-the-most-expensive-childcare/; "Public Spending on Childcare and Early Education," Paris, France: OECD Family database, Social Policy Division, www.oecd.org/els/ soc/PF3_1_Public_spending_on_childcare_and_early_education.pdf.

105. Jason Beckfield and Clare Bambra, "Shorter Lives in Stingier States: Social Policy Shortcomings Help Explain the US Mortality Disadvantage," *Social Science & Medicine* 171 (December 2016): 30–38. www.sciencedirect.com/ science/article/pii/S0277953616305858.

106. Valerie Wilson and Jessica Schieder, "Countries Investing More in Social Programs Have Less Child Poverty," Economic Policy Institute, June 1, 2018, www.epi.org/publication/ countries-investing-more-in-social-programs-have-less-child-poverty.

107. Maria T. Carney et al., "Elder Orphans Hiding in Plain Sight: A Growing Vulnerable Population," *Current Gerontology and Geriatrics Research* (October 23, 2016): 1–11, https://doi.org/10.1155/2016/4723250.

108. *A Profile of Older Americans: 2015*, Administration on Aging, Administration for Community Living (U.S. Department of Health and Human Services, 2015), https://acl.gov/sites/default/files/Aging%20and%20 Disability%20in%20America/2015-Profile.pdf.

109. Karen Shellenback, *Child Care & Parent Productivity: Making the Business Case* (Ithaca, NY: Cornell University, 2004), http://s3.amazonaws.com/mildredwarner.org/attachments/000/000/074/original/154-21008542.pdf.

110. Heidi Shierholz, "Paid Leave Is Good for Business," *Better Workplaces, Better Businesses.* (blog), U.S. Department of Labor, December 19, 2014, http://betterwbb.org/paid-leave-good-business.

111. Francine D. Blau and Lawrence M. Kahn, "Female Labor Supply: Why Is the US Falling Behind?" *American Economic Review* 103, no. 3, (2013): 251–256, www.nber.org/papers/w18702; Leah Ruppanner, Stephanie Moller, and Liana Sayer, "Expensive Childcare and Short School Days = Lower Maternal Employment and More Time in Childcare? Evidence from the American Time Use Survey," *Socius: Sociological Research for a Dynamic World* 5 (2019): 1–14, https://journals.sagepub.com/doi/pdf/10.1177/2378023119860277.

112. "Breadwinner Moms," Pew Research Center, May 29, 2013, www.pewsocialtrends.org/2013/05/29/ breadwinner-moms.

113. Leila Schochet, *The Child Care Crisis Is Keeping Women Out of the Workforce*, Center for American Progress, March 28, 2019, www.americanprogress.org/issues/early-childhood/reports/2019/03/28/467488/ child-care-crisis-keeping-women-workforce.

114. Rasheed Malik, "The Effects of Universal Preschool in Washington, D.C.," Center for American Progress, September 26, 2018, www.americanprogress.org/issues/early-childhood/reports/2018/09/26/458208/ effects-universal-preschool-washington-d-c.

115. Allison Daminger, "The Cognitive Dimension of Household Labor," *American Sociological Review* 84, no. 4 (July 9, 2019): 609–633, https://journals.sagepub.com/doi/abs/10.1177/0003122419859007?journalCode=asra.

116. McKinsey Global Institute, *The Power of Parity: How Advancing Women's Equality Can Add $12 Trillion To Global Growth* (New York: McKinsey Global Institute, 2015), www.mckinsey.com/~/media/McKinsey/Featured%20 Insights/Employment%20and%20Growth/How%20advancing%20womens%20equality%20can%20add%20 12%20trillion%20to%20global%20growth/MGI%20Power%20of%20parity_Full%20report_September%20 2015.ashx.

117. Juliana Menasce Horowitz et al, "Americans Widely Support Paid Family and Medical Leave but Differ Over Specific Policies," Pew Research Center, March 23, 2017, www.pewsocialtrends.org/2017/03/23/ americans-widely-support-paid-family-and-medical-leave-but-differ-over-specific-policies.

CHAPTER FIVE

118. "Percentage of Children from Birth through Age 5 and Not Yet in Kindergarten Participating in Weekly Nonparental Care," National Household Education Surveys Program (NHES), National Center for Education Statistics, Institute of Education Sciences, 2016, https://nces.ed.gov/nhes/tables/ECPP_HoursPerWeek_Care.asp.

119. Margaret Meade, *Culture and Commitment: A Study of the Generation Gap* (London: The Bodley Head, 1975), 72.

120. Chris M. Herbst, "Universal Child Care, Maternal Employment, and Children's Long-Run Outcomes: Evidence from the U.S. Lanham Act of 1940," IZA, December 2013, http://ftp.iza.org/dp7846.pdf.

121. Deborah A. Phillips et al., "Puzzling It Out: The Current State of Scientific Knowledge on Pre-Kindergarten Effects," in *The Current State of Scientific Knowledge on Pre-Kindergarten Effects* (Washington, DC: The Brookings Institution Press, 2017), 1–106, www.brookings.edu/wp-content/uploads/2017/04/duke_prekstudy _final_4-4-17_hires.pdf.

122. Jorge Luis García, James J. Heckman, Duncan Ermini Leaf, and María José Prados, "The Life-Cycle Benefits of an Influential Early Childhood Program," National Bureau of Economic Research, Working Paper 22993, 2016, www.nber.org/papers/w22993.pdf.

123. Juliana Menasce Horowitz et al., 4. Gender and Caregiving "Americans Widely Support Paid Family and Medical Leave, But Differ Over Specific Policies," Pew Research Center, May 23, 2017, www.pewsocialtrends .org/2017/03/23/gender-and-caregiving.

124. Anne Mitchell, Louise Stoney, and Harriet Dichter, *Financing Child Care in the United States: An Expanded Catalog of Current Strategies* (Kansas City, MO: Ewing Marion Kauffman Foundation, 2001), https://files.eric .ed.gov/fulltext/ED458932.pdf.

125. Nikki Graf, "Most Americans Say Children Are Better Off with a Parent at Home," Pew Research Center, October 10, 2016, www.pewresearch.org/fact-tank/2016/10/10/most-americans-say-children-are -better-off-with-a-parent-at-home.

126. Nancy L. Cohen, "Why America Never Had Universal Child Care: In 1971, a National Day-Care Bill Almost Became Law. Therein Lies a Story," The New Republic, April 24, 2013, https://newrepublic.com/article/113009 /child-care-america-was-very-close-universal-day-care.

127. Nikki Graf, "Most Americans Say Children Are Better Off with a Parent at Home," Pew Research Center, October 10, 2016, www.pewresearch.org/fact-tank/2016/10/10/most-americans-say-children-are -better-off-with-a-parent-at-home.

128. Jen Gann, "6 Women on How They've Been Treated at Work After Having Kids," The Cut, June 13, 2018, www .thecut.com/2018/06/6-women-pregnancy-discrimination-motherhood-workplace.html.

129. Lisa Oppenheimer, "For Millennial Parents, Child Care Is Only Part of the Answer," Bright Horizons, 2020, www.brighthorizons.com/employer-resources/millennial-parents.

130. Eva Landsberg, Marc Tucker, and Sharon Lynn Kagan, *The Early Advantage 2: Building Systems That Work for Young Children: International Insights from Innovative Early Childhood Systems* (New York: Teachers College Press, 2019).

131. Johannes Bos et al., *Connecting All Children to High-Quality Early Care and Education: Promising Strategies from the International Community* (Washington, DC: American Institute for Research, 2016), www.air.org/system/files /downloads/report/High-Quality-Early-Care-and-Education-International-October-2016.pdf.

132. Organisation for Economic Co-operation and Development, *Education at a Glance, 2016* (Paris: OECD Publishing, 2016), www.oecd-ilibrary.org/education/education-at-a-glance-2016_eag-2016-en.

133. Comparable data across nations is difficult to access, especially since the United States has such a variety of programs and funding sources for early childhood education. However, to glimpse further into enrollment data, note that in 2020, Head Start preschools served only 36 percent of eligible children ages three to five years old and 11 percent of eligible children under three. NHSA, "2020 National Head Start Profile," National Head Start Association, 2020, https://nhsa.app.box.com/s/ln2yxypq1ux2v5hw8bpn6l7auzstrmir/file/604151683181. Similarly, NIEER reports that about a third of the nation's four-year-olds were enrolled in state-funded preschool programs nationwide during the 2017–18 school year, an increase of about 35,000 children from the previous year. At the current rate of growth, it would take twenty years for state preschool programs to have enough seats to enroll half of the nation's four-year-olds; Allison H. Friedman-Krauss et al., *The State of Preschool 2018: State Preschool Yearbook* (New Brunswick, NJ: National Institute for Early Education Research, 2019), http://nieer.org /wp-content/uploads/2019/08/YB2018_Full-ReportR3wAppendices.pdf.

134. "Parenting in America: Outlook, Worries, Aspirations Are Strongly Linked to Financial Situation," Pew Research Center, December 17, 2015, www.pewsocialtrends.org/2015/12/17/parenting-in-america.

135. "2017 National Poll," First Five Years Fund, www.ffyf.org/2017-poll.

136. Rasheed Malik et al., "Child Care Deserts: An Analysis of Child Care Centers by ZIP Code in 8 States," Center for American Progress, October 27, 2016, www.americanprogress.org/issues/early-childhood/reports/2016/10 /27/225703/child-care-deserts.

137. "Parenting in America: Outlook, Worries, Aspirations Are Strongly Linked to Financial Situation," Pew Research Center, December 17, 2015, www.pewsocialtrends.org/2015/12/17/parenting-in-america.

138. Julia Mendez and Danielle Crosby, "Why and How Do Low-Income Hispanic Families Search for Early Care and Education (ECE)?" Hispanic Research Center, May 2018, www.hispanicresearchcenter.org/wp-content /uploads/2019/08/Hispanics-Center-parental-search-brief-5.16-V21.pdf; Milagros Nores, "Early Childhood Choices and Hispanic Families," National Institute for Early Education Research, 2016, http://nieer.org/wp-content/uploads/2016/08/Early20childhood20choices20and20Hispanic20families.pdf.

139. Rasheed Malik et al., "Child Care Deserts: An Analysis of Child Care Centers by ZIP Code in 8 States," Center for American Progress, October 27, 2016, www.americanprogress.org/issues/early-childhood/reports/2016/10 /27/225703/child-care-deserts.

140. Jeffrey Capizzano and Gina Adams, "The Number of Child Care Arrangements Used by Children Under Five: Variation Across States," Washington DC: The Urban Institute, March 2000, http://webarchive.urban.org /UploadedPDF/anf_b12.pdf; Rasheed Malik, "Working Families Are Spending Big Money on Child Care," Center for American Progress, June 20, 2019, https://cdn.americanprogress.org/content/uploads/2019 /06/19074131/Working-Families-SpendingBRIEF.pdf.

141. Anna Bahney, "Child Care Is Biggest Expense for a Growing Number of Families," *Forbes*, June 29, 2015, www.forbes.com/sites/annabahney/2015/06/29/child-care-is-biggest-expense-for -a-growing-number-of-families/#3097cdf4e8ad.

142. Lindsay Oncken, "The First Pillar of Care: Cost," New America, September 16, 2016, www.newamerica.org /in-depth/care-report/first-pillar-care-cost.

143. Brigid Schulte, "Parents Miss Work, Lose Jobs Trying to Get Child-Care Subsidy," *Washington Post*, May 15, 2013, www.washingtonpost.com/local/parents-miss-work-lose-jobs-trying-to-get-child-care-subsidy/2013/05/15/3031ac2c-ba59-11e2-b94c-b684dda07add_story.html; Valora Washington and Mary Reed, "A Study of the Massachusetts Child Care Voucher System: Impact on Children, Families, Providers, and Resource and Referral Agencies," *Families in Society* 89, no. 2 (April–June 2008): 202–207, https://doi.org/10.1606%2F1044-3894.3735.

144. Susannah Howe, "The Second Pillar of Care: Quality," New America, September 16, 2016, www.newamerica.org /in-depth/care-report/second-pillar-care-quality.

145. "Benchmarks for High-Quality Pre-K Checklist," NIEER, http://nieer.org/wp-content/uploads/2019/12 /BENCHMARKS-CHECK-LIST-PDF.pdf.

146. National Institute of Child Health and Human Development, *The NICHD Study of Early Child Care and Youth Development—Findings for Children up to Age 4 1/2 Years*, NIH Pub. No. 05-4318 (U.S. Department of Health and Human Services, National Institutes Of Health, 2006), www.nichd.nih.gov/sites/default/files/publications /pubs/documents/seccyd_06.pdf.

147. Alison Kodjak, "What Makes for Quality Child Care? It Depends Whom You Ask," NPR, October 18, 2016, www.npr.org/sections/health-shots/2016/10/18/498255186/what-makes-for-quality-child-care-it-depends-who-you-ask.

148. Lindsay Oncken, "The First Pillar of Care: Cost," New America, September 16, 2016, www.newamerica.org /in-depth/care-report/first-pillar-care-cost.

149. "2015 State Fact Sheets," Arlington, VA: ChildCare Aware of America, 2015, www.childcareaware.org /wp-content/uploads/2015/10/StateFactSheets_intro.pdf.

150. Jim Squires, "Preschool Matters Today: Rethinking the Numbers," NIEER, http://nieer.org/2017/02/17 /rethinking-the-numbers; NAEYC, "The 10 NAEYC Program Standards," National Association for the Education of Youth Children, February 17, 2017, www.naeyc.org/our-work/families/10-naeyc-program-standards.

151. Marcy Whitebook, Caitlin McLean, and Lea J.E. Austin, *Early Childhood Workforce Index—2016* (Berkeley: Center for the Study of Child Care Employment, University of California, 2016), https://cscce.berkeley.edu /files/2016/Early-Childhood-Workforce-Index-2016.pdf; Marcy Whitebook, Caitlin McLean, and Lea J.E. Austin, "Executive Summary: Early Childhood Workforce Index," https://cscce.berkeley.edu/files/2016/Index-2016-Executive-Summary.pdf; "Occupational Employment and Wages, May 2019: 39-9011 Childcare Workers," US Bureau of Labor Statistics, https://www.bls.gov/oes/current/oes399011.htm.

152. Marcy Whitebook, Caitlin McLean, and Lea J.E. Austin, *Early Childhood Workforce Index—2016* (Berkeley: Center for the Study of Child Care Employment, University of California, 2016), https://cscce.berkeley.edu/ files/2016/Early-Childhood-Workforce-Index-2016.pdf; Marcy Whitebook and Laura Sakai, *Turnover Begets Turnover: An Examination of Job and Occupational Instability Among Child Care Center Staff* (Berkeley: Institute of Industrial Relations, Center for the Study of Child Care Employment, 2003).

153. "High-Quality Early Learning Settings Depend on a High-Quality Workforce: Low Compensation Undermines Quality," U.S. Department of Health and Human Services, U.S. Department of Education, June 2016, https:// www2.ed.gov/about/inits/ed/earlylearning/files/ece-low-compensation-undermines-quality-report-2016.pdf.

154. Marcy Whitebook, Caitlin McLean, and Lea J.E. Austin, *Early Childhood Workforce Index—2016* (Berkeley: Center for the Study of Child Care Employment, University of California, 2016), https://cscce.berkeley.edu /files/2016/Early-Childhood-Workforce-Index-2016.pdf.

155. Brené Brown, "The Power of Vulnerability," TEDxHouston, June 2010, www.ted.com/talks/brene_brown _the_power_of_vulnerability/transcript.

156. "Erika Huggins: The Official Website," www.erickahuggins.com.

157. "Martin Luther King on Love and Power," https://youtu.be/U0uEVTh0ios.

CHAPTER SIX

158. Olga Khazan, "How Parents Around the World Describe Their Children, in Charts," *The Atlantic*, April 12, 2013, www.theatlantic.com/international/archive/2013/04/how-parents-around-the -world-describe-their-children-in-charts/274955.

159. Amy S. Choi, "How Cultures around the World Think about Parenting," Ideas.TED.com, July 15, 2014, https:// ideas.ted.com/how-cultures-around-the-world-think-about-parenting.

160. Abraham Lincoln, *Lincoln: Speeches and Writings: 1859–1865, Volume 2* (Norwalk, CT: Heritage Illustrated Publishing, 2014).

161. Barack Obama, "Second Inaugural Speech," the White House archives, https://obamawhitehouse.archives.gov /the-press-office/2013/01/21/inaugural-address-president-barack-obama.

162. Cristina Novoa, "Opportunities for States to Improve Infant Health Outcomes," Center for American Progress, December 17, 2019, https://cdn.americanprogress.org/content/uploads/2019/12/11120006/Infant-Health-Disparities-BRIEF.pdf.

163. UNICEF Office of Research, "Building the Future: Children and the Sustainable Development Goals in Rich Countries," Innocenti Report Card 14, UNICEF Office of Research, 2017, www.unicef-irc.org/publications/pdf /RC14_eng.pdf, 12–13.

164. Saki Knafo, "U.S. Child Poverty Second Highest Among Developed Nations: Report," Huffington Post, May 31, 2012, www.huffpost.com/entry/us-child-poverty-report-unicef_n_1555533.

165. Eric A. Hanushek et al., "Long-Run Trends in the U.S. SES-Achievement Gap," Harvard Kennedy School, Program on Education Policy and Governance Working Papers Series, Cambridge, 2020, www.hks.harvard.edu /sites/default/files/Taubman/PEPG/research/PEPG20_01.pdf.

166. Valerie Wilson and Jessica Schieder, "Countries Investing More in Social Programs Have Less Child Poverty," Economic Policy Institute, June 1, 2018, www.epi.org/publication/countries-investing-more-in -social-programs-have-less-child-poverty.

167. National Academies of Sciences, Engineering, and Medicine. *A Roadmap to Reducing Child Poverty* (Washington, DC: The National Academies Press, 2019), 6.

168. Sharon Lynn Kagan, "Dreaming Big and Acting Smart: A Study of Six Nations Led by TC's Sharon Lynn Kagan Distills Principles for Improving Early Childhood Education and Care," Teachers College, Columbia University, 2019, www.tc.columbia.edu/articles/2019/may/dreaming-big-and-acting-smart/; Eva Landsberg, Marc Tucker, and Sharon Lynn Kagan, *The Early Advantage 2: Building Systems That Work for Young Children: International Insights from Innovative Early Childhood Systems*, New York: Teachers College Press, 2019.

169. Leslie Boissiere et al., *Race for Results* (Baltimore: Annie E. Casey Foundation, 2017), www.aecf.org/m /resourcedoc/aecf-2017raceforresults-2017.pdf.

170. Bridget Ansel, "Failing to Invest in Young Kids Is Damaging the U.S. Economy," Washington Center for Equitable Growth, January 17, 2017, https://equitablegrowth.org/failing-to-invest-in -young-kids-is-damaging-the-u-s-economy.

171. Danielle M. Ely and Anne K. Driscoll, "Infant Mortality in the United States, 2017: Data from the Period Linked Birth/Infant Death File," *National Vital Statistics Reports* 68, no. 10 (August 1, 2019), www.cdc.gov/nchs/data /nvsr/nvsr68/nvsr68_10-508.pdf.

172. "Children in Poverty," Child Trends Databank, January 28, 2019, www.childtrends.org/?indicators=children -in-poverty.

173. Valerie Wilson and Jessica Schieder, "The Rise in Child Poverty Reveals Racial Inequality, More Than a Failed War on Poverty," Economic Policy Institute, June 8, 2018, www.epi.org/publication/the-rise-in-child-poverty-reveals -racial-inequality-more-than-a-failed-war-on-poverty.

174. "Thirty-Five Percent of Fourth-Graders at or Above NAEP Proficient Lower Compared to 2017," The Nation's Report Card National Average Scores 2019, www.nationsreportcard.gov/reading/nation/achievement/?grade=4.

175. "Racial and Ethnic Achievement Gaps," The Educational Opportunity Monitoring Project, Stanford Center for Education Policy Analysis, https://cepa.stanford.edu/educational-opportunity-monitoring-project/achievement-gaps/race.

176. Roland Fryer and Steven D. Levitt, "Falling Behind: New Evidence on the Black-White Achievement Gap," *EducationNext* 4, no. 4 (Fall 2004): 1–4, www.educationnext.org/fallingbehind.

177. Otto Kerner et al., *Report of the National Advisory Commission on Civil Disorders* (Washington, DC: U.S. Department of Justice or the National Criminal Justice Reference Service, 1968), www.ncjrs.gov/pdffiles1/Digitization/8073NCJRS.pdf.

178. James S. Coleman et al., *Equality of Educational Opportunity* (Washington, DC: U.S. Department of Health, Education, and Welfare, 1966), https://files.eric.ed.gov/fulltext/ED012275.pdf.

179. Linda Darling-Hammond, "From 'Separate but Equal' to 'No Child Left Behind,'" in Eleanor Blair Hilty, *Thinking about Schools* (New York: Routledge, 2018), 419–437, https://doi.org/10.4324/9780429495670-34; Linda Darling-Hammond, "Evaluating 'No Child Left Behind,'" *The Nation*, May 2, 2007, www.thenation.com/article/archive/evaluating-no-child-left-behind; Linda Darling-Hammond, "Race, Inequality and Educational Accountability: The Irony of 'No Child Left Behind,'" *Race Ethnicity and Education* 10, no. 3 (October 18, 2007): 245–260, https://doi.org/10.1080/13613320701503207.

180. "Every Student Succeeds Act (ESSA)," First Five Years Fund, https://www.ffyf.org/issues/essa/; Lauren Mendoza, "46 States and Territories to Receive Preschool Development Grants," First Five Years Fund, January 4, 2019, www.ffyf.org/45-states-and-territories-to-receive-preschool-development-grants/?mc_cid=7323d113ad&mc_eid=2ba37ccf10&mc_cid=03c1f84c73&mc_eid=142e14e4d6.

181. *K–12 Education: Better Use of Information Could Help Agencies Identify Disparities and Address Racial Discrimination* (Washington, DC: Government Accountability Office, 2016), www.gao.gov/assets/680/676745.pdf.

182. James S. Coleman et al., *Equality of Educational Opportunity* (Washington, DC: U.S. Department of Health, Education, and Welfare, 1966), 619, http://files.eric.ed.gov/fulltext/ED012275.pdf.

183. Peter Piazza and Erica Frankenberg, "Segregation at an Early Age, 2019 Update," Center for Education and Civil Rights, Penn State, November 2019, https://cecr.ed.psu.edu/sites/default/files/Segregation_At_An_Early_Age_Piazza_Frankenberg_2019.pdf, 1–2.

184. Andrew R. Todd, Kelsey C. Thiem, and Rebecca Neel, "Does Seeing Faces of Young Black Boys Facilitate the Identification of Threatening Stimuli?" *Psychological Science* 27, no. 12 (2016): 384–393 and 1673. https://doi.org/10.1177/0956797615624492; "Faces of Black Children as Young as Five Evoke Negative Biases," *Association for Psychologial Science,* February 8, 2016, www.psychologicalscience.org/news/releases/faces-of-black-children-as-young-as-five-evoke-negative-biases.html.

185. Maithreyi Gopalan and Ashlyn Aiko Nelson, "Understanding the Racial Discipline Gap in Schools," *AERA Open* 5, no. 2 (April 1, 2019): 1–26, https://journals.sagepub.com/doi/10.1177/2332858419844613. FFrancis A. Pearman et al., "Are Achievement Gaps Related to Discipline Gaps? Evidence from National Data," *AERA Open* 5, no. 4 (October 1, 2019): 1–18, https://doi.org/10.1177/2332858419875440. Mark Alden Morgan and John Paul Wright, "Beyond Black and White: Suspension Disparities for Hispanic, Asian, and White Youth," *Criminal Justice Review* 43, no. 4 (July 21, 2017): 377–398, https://doi.org/10.1177/0734016817721293.

186. Rebecca Epstein, Jamilia Blake, and Thalia González, "Girlhood Interrupted: The Erasure of Black Girls' Childhood," SSRN, July 18, 2017, https://ssrn.com/abstract=3000695; Rebecca Epstein and Jamilia Blake, "Listening to Black Women and Girls: Lived Experiences of Adultification Bias," The Georgetown Law Center on Poverty and Inequality, May 15, 2019, www.law.georgetown.edu/news/research-confirms-that-black-girls-feel-the-sting-of-adultification-bias-identified-in-earlier-georgetown-law-study.

187. Dan Goldhaber, Lesley Lavery, and Roddy Theobald, "Uneven Playing Field? Assessing the Teacher Quality Gap Between Advantaged and Disadvantaged Students," *Educational Researcher* 44, no. 5 (June 1, 2015): 293–307, https://doi.org/10.3102/0013189X15592622.

188. Ronald F. Ferguson, "Paying for Public Education: New Evidence on How and Why Money Matters," *Harvard Journal on Legislation* 28, no. 2 (Summer 1991): 465–498.

189. Francis A. Pearman, F. Chris Curran, Benjamin Fisher, and Joseph Gardella, "Are Achievement Gaps Related to Discipline Gaps? Evidence from National Data," *AERA Open* 5, no. 4 (October–December 2019): 1–18, https://journals.sagepub.com/doi/pdf/10.1177/2332858419875440.

190. Linda Darling-Hammond, "Inequality in Teaching and Schooling: How Opportunity Is Rationed to Students of Color in America," in *The Right Thing to Do, the Smart Thing to Do: Enhancing Diversity in the Health Professions: Summary of the Symposium on Diversity in Health Professions in Honor of Herbert W. Nickens, M.D.* (Washington, DC: National Academies Press, 2001), www.ncbi.nlm.nih.gov/books/NBK223640.

191. "$23 Billion" (Jersey City, New Jersey: EdBuild, 2019), https://edbuild.org/content/23-billion/full-report.pdf.

192. Darien Wynn, "Underrepresentation of High-Achieving Students of Color in Gifted Programs," Thomas B. Fordham Institute, February 17, 2016, https://fordhaminstitute.org/national/commentary /underrepresentation-high-achieving-students-color-gifted-programs.

193. Jason A. Grissom and Christopher Redding, "Discretion and Disproportionality: Explaining the Underrepresentation of High-Achieving Students of Color in Gifted Programs," *AERA Open* 2, no. 1 (January 8, 2016), https://doi.org/10.1177/2332858415622175.

194. The Hechinger Report, "Bright Black Students with Black Teachers More Likely to Get into Gifted Programs," *U.S. News*, January 19, 2016, www.usnews.com/news/articles/2016-01-19/bright-black-students-with -black-teachers-more-likely-to-get-into-gifted-programs.

195. Dan Goldhaber, Roddy Theobald, and Christopher Tien, "The Theoretical and Empirical Arguments for Diversifying the Teacher Workforce: A Review of the Evidence," Center for Education Data and Research, 2015, http://m.cedr.us/papers/working/CEDR%20WP%202015-9.pdf.

196. Horace Mann, *Twelfth Annual Report to the Secretary of the Massachusetts State Board of Education*, (Commonwealth of Massachusetts: Board of Education, 1848), 59, https://archives.lib.state.ma.us/handle /2452/204731.

197. Linda Darling-Hammond, "Inequality in Teaching and Schooling: How Opportunity Is Rationed to Students of Color in America," in *The Right Thing to Do, the Smart Thing to Do: Enhancing Diversity in the Health Professions: Summary of the Symposium on Diversity in Health Professions in Honor of Herbert W. Nickens, M.D.* (Washington, DC: National Academies Press, 2001), www.ncbi.nlm.nih.gov/books/NBK223640.

198. Julia B. Isaacs, Isabel V. Sawhill, and Ron Haskins, *Getting Ahead or Losing Ground: Economic Mobility in America* (Washington, DC: The Brookings Institution, 2016), 7 www.brookings.edu/wp-content/uploads/2016/06 /02_economic_mobility_sawhill.pdf.

199. Nellie Bowles, "Human Contact Is Now a Luxury Good: Screens Used to Be for the Elite. Now Avoiding Them Is a Status Symbol," *New York Times*, March 23, 2019, www.nytimes.com/2019/03/23/sunday-review/human -contact-luxury-screens.html.

200. Naomi Schafer Riley, "The Real Digital Divide Isn't about Access to the Internet," *Washington Post*, April 18, 2019, www.washingtonpost.com/opinions/2019/04/18/real-digital-divide-isnt-about-access-internet.

201. Organisation for Economic Co-operation and Development, *A Broken Social Elevator? How to Promote Social Mobility* (Paris: OCED Publishing, 2018), https://doi.org/10.1787/9789264301085-en.

202. Eric A. Hanushek, "What Matters for Achievement: Updating Coleman on the Influence of Families and Schools," *Education Next* 16, no. 2 (Spring 2016): 22–30.

203. Allison H. Friedman-Krauss et al., *The State of Preschool 2018: State Preschool Yearbook* (New Brunswick, NJ: National Institute for Early Education Research, 2019), http://nieer.org/wp-content/uploads/2019/08/YB2018_ Full-ReportR3wAppendices.pdf.

204. P. Lindsay Chase-Lansdale and Jeanne Brooks-Gunn, "Two-Generation Programs in the Twenty-First Century," *The Future of Children* 24, no. 1 (Spring 2014): 14, https://files.eric.ed.gov/fulltext/EJ1029028.pdf.

205. Ron Haskins, Irwin Garfinkel, and Sara McLanahan, "Introduction: Two-Generation Mechanisms of Child Development," *The Future of Children* 24, no. 1 (Spring 2014): 3–12, doi:10.1353/foc.2014.0001.

206. Gilbert Y. Steiner, *The Children's Cause* (Washington, DC: Brookings Institution, 1976), 118.

207. Rob Reiner, "Parents' Action for Children," The Huffington Post, May 26, 2005, www.huffpost.com/entry /parents-action-for-childr_b_1430.

CHAPTER SEVEN

208. Ronald Reagan, "Speech of the Former President at the 1992 Republican Convention," American History, www .let.rug.nl/usa/presidents/ronald-wilson-reagan/speech-of-the-former-president-at-the-1992-republican- convention.php http://www.let.rug.nl/usa/presidents/ronald-wilson-reagan/speech-of-the-former-president-at-the -1992-republican-convention.php.

209. Holly Green, "Are You Bold?" *Forbes,* January 31, 2012, www.forbes.com/sites/work-in-progress/2012/01/31 /are-you-bold/#646fff566355.

210. Hannah Hartig and Hannah Gilberstadt, "Younger Americans More Likely Than Older Adults to Say There Are Other Countries That Are Better Than the U.S.," Pew Research Center, January 8, 2020,www.pewresearch.org /fact-tank/2020/01/08/younger-americans-more-likely-than-older-adults-to-say-there-are-other-countries-that-are -better-than-the-u-s.

211. Jay Ogilvy, "Scenario Planning and Strategic Forecasting," *Forbes*, January 8, 2015, www.forbes.com/sites /stratfor/2015/01/08/scenario-planning-and-strategic-forecasting/#661c29af411a.

212. Section 4: Views of the Nation "The Generation Gap and the 2012 Election," Pew Research Center, November 3, 2011, www.people-press.org/2011/11/03/section-4-views-of-the-nation/?src=prc-number.

213. John Dickinson, *The Political Writings of John Dickinson, Esquire: The Speech of John Dickinson . . . May 24th, 1764 . . . Praying the King for a Change of the Government of the Province* (Seattle, WA: Palala Press, 2016).

214. Valora Washington, Brenda Gadson, and Kathryn Amel, *The New Early Childhood Professional: A Step-by-Step Guide to Overcoming Goliath* (New York: Teachers College Press, 2015), 88–89.

215. Quoted in Lillian Mongeau, "Who Should Pay for Preschool for the Middle Class?: Universal Preschool Has a Significant Positive Effect on Reading Scores of Children from Low-Income Homes, But Programs Targeted to Poor Children Do Not," The Hechinger Report, June 25, 2018, https://hechingerreport.org/who-should-pay -for-preschool.

216. Elliot Haspel, *Crawling Behind: America's Child Care Crisis and How to Fix It* (Castroville, TX: Black Rose Writing, 2019) quoted in Claire Cain Miller, "Public School Is a Child's Right. Should Preschool Be Also?" *New York Times,* March 15, 2020.

217. James Heckman and Henry Schultz, "Invest in the Very Young," in *Encyclopedia on Early Childhood Development*, eds. R. E. Tremblay, M. Boivin, RDeV Peters, updated March 2011, www.child-encyclopedia.com/importance -early-childhood-development/according-experts/invest-very-young.

218. Stacie G. Goffin and Valora Washington, *Ready or Not: Early Care and Education's Leadership Choices—12 Years Later*, 2nd ed. (New York: Teachers College Press, 2019).

219. Stacie G. Goffin and Valora Washington, *Ready or Not: Early Care and Education's Leadership Choices—12 Years Later*, 2nd ed. (New York: Teachers College Press, 2019).

220. John Haplin, Karl Agne, and Margie Omero, "Affordable Child Care and Early Learning for All Families: A National Public Opinion Study," Center for American Progress, September 13, 2018, www.americanprogress.org /issues/early-childhood/reports/2018/09/13/457470/affordable-child-care-early-learning-families.

221. Reid Wilson, "Americans Pessimistic about Country's Future: Survey," The Hill, March 21, 2019, https://thehill .com/homenews/state-watch/435051-americans-pessimistic-about-countrys-future-survey.

222. "Key Takeaways on Americans' Views of and Experiences with Family and Medical Leave," Pew Research Center, March 23, 2017, www.pewresearch.org/fact-tank/2017/03/23/key-takeaways-on -americans-views-of-and-experiences-with-family-and-medical-leave.

223. Warren Bennis, *The Essential Bennis* (San Francisco: Jossey-Bass Publishers, 2015), 106.

224. Julián Castro, "Julián Castro DNC Speech (Text, Video)," Politico, September 4, 2012, www.politico.com /story/2012/09/julian-castro-dnc-speech-text-video-080691.

225. Valora Washington and Lisa Yarkony, "Child Care for All: Finding the Will and the Way," Council for Professional Recognition, February 2019, www.cdacouncil.org/storage/documents/Media_Room/Child_Care_for_All.pdf.

CHAPTER EIGHT

226. Margaret Mead, *People and Places* (New York: Bantam Pathfinder Editions, 1959), 198.

227. Charles Handy, *Tocqueville Revisited: The Meaning of American Prosperity* (Boston: Harvard Business Review, 2001), https://hbr.org/2001/01/tocqueville-revisited-the-meaning-of-american-prosperity.

228. "Real Clear Opinion Research," Real Clear Politics.com, February 22–26, 2019, www.realclearpolitics.com /docs/190305_RCOR_Topline_V2.pdf; Carl M. Cannon and Tom Bevan, "The American Dream: Not Dead — Yet," www.realclearpolitics.com/articles/2019/03/06/the_american_dream_not_dead_--_yet_139659.html.

229. *Life Experiences and Income Inequality in the United States*, NPR, January 2020, https://apps.npr.org /documents/document.html?id=6603517-Income-Inequality-Report-January-2020; Danielle Kurtzleben, "Richest Republicans View Health Care Far Differently Than Poorest, NPR Poll Finds," NPR, January 9, 2020, www.npr .org/2020/01/09/789127994/npr-poll-finds-sizable-income-gap-on-republicans-views-of-health-coverage.

230. John F. Kennedy, "John F. Kennedy Moon Speech—Rice Stadium, September 12, 1962," National Aeronautics and Space Administration, https://er.jsc.nasa.gov/seh/ricetalk.htm.

231. Barack Obama, "Barack Obama's Caucus Speech," *New York Times*, January 3, 2008, www.nytimes.com /2008/01/03/us/politics/03obama-transcript.html.

232. Jean M. Twenge, Ryne A. Sherman, and Sonja Lyubomirsky, "More Happiness for Young People and Less for Mature Adults: Time Period Differences in Subjective Well-Being in the United States, 1972–2014," *Social Psychological and Personality Science* 7, no. 2, (2016): 131–141, https://doi.org/10.1177/1948550615602933.

233. John F. Helliwell et al., *World Happiness Report 2020* (New York: United Nations Sustainable Development Solutions Network, 2020), https://worldhappiness.report/ed/2020/#read.

234. *Life Experiences and Income Inequality in the United States*, National Public Radio, January 2020, https://apps.npr.org/documents/document.html?id=6603517-Income-Inequality-Report-January-2020; Danielle Kurtzleben, "Richest Republicans View Health Care Far Differently Than Poorest, NPR Poll Finds," NPR, January 9, 2020, www.npr.org/2020/01/09/789127994/npr-poll-finds-sizable-income-gap-on-republicans-views-of-health-coverage.

235. *Life Experiences and Income Inequality in the United States*, National Public Radio, January 2020, https://apps.npr.org/documents/document.html?id=6603517-Income-Inequality-Report-January-2020.

236. "Real Clear Opinion Research," Real Clear Politics.com, February 22–26, 2019, www.realclearpolitics.com/docs/190305_RCOR_Topline_V2.pdf; Carl M. Cannon and Tom Bevan, "The American Dream: Not Dead — Yet," www.realclearpolitics.com/articles/2019/03/06/the_american_dream_not_dead_--_yet_139659.html.

237. Elizabeth Mendes, "In U.S., Optimism about Future for Youth Reaches All-Time Low: The Highest-Income Americans Are Among the Least Optimistic about the Future," Gallup, May 2, 2011, https://news.gallup.com/poll/147350/optimism-future-youth-reaches-time-low.aspx.

238. Alessandra Malito, "Only 37% of Americans Believe Today's Children Will Grow Up to Be Better Off," MarketWatch, August 23, 2017, www.marketwatch.com/story/only-37-of-americans-believe-todays-children-will-grow-up-to-be-better-off-2017-08-22; Chapter 3. Inequality and Economic Mobility, "Economies of Emerging Markets Better Rated During Difficult Times" Pew Research Center, May 23, 2013, www.pewresearch.org/global/2013/05/23/chapter-3-inequality-and-economic-mobility/#real-divisions-in-faithin-economic-mobility?mod=article_inline.

239. Alessandra Malito, "Only 37% of Americans Believe Today's Children Will Grow Up to Be Better Off," MarketWatch, August 23, 2017, www.marketwatch.com/story/only-37-of-americans-believe-todays-children-will-grow-up-to-be-better-off-2017-08-22.

240. Kim Parker, Rich Morin, and Juliana Menasce Horowitz, "Looking to the Future, Public Sees an America in Decline on Many Fronts," Pew Research Center, March 21, 2019, www.pewsocialtrends.org/2019/03/21/public-sees-an-america-in-decline-on-many-fronts.

241. Kim Parker, Rich Morin, and Juliana Menasce Horowitz, "Looking to the Future, Public Sees an America in Decline on Many Fronts," Pew Research Center, March 21, 2019, www.pewsocialtrends.org/2019/03/21/public-sees-an-america-in-decline-on-many-fronts.

242. William J. Clinton, "First Inaugural Address of William J. Clinton; January 20, 1993," The Avalon Project at Yale Law School, https://avalon.law.yale.edu/20th_century/clinton1.asp.

243. *2018 Grandparents Today National Survey: General Population Report* (Washington, DC: American Association of Retired Persons, 2019), www.aarp.org/content/dam/aarp/research/surveys_statistics/life-leisure/2019/aarp-grandparenting-study.doi.10.26419-2Fres.00289.001.pdf.

244. Franklin D. Roosevelt, "Address on Hemisphere Defense, Dayton, Ohio, October 12, 1940," The American Presidency Project at UC Santa Barbara, www.presidency.ucsb.edu/documents/address-hemisphere-defense-dayton-ohio.

245. John Paul XXIII, "Quotes by Popes," JesuitResource.org, Xavier University, www.xavier.edu/jesuitresource/online-resources/quote-archive1/pope-quotes.

246. Sheila Quirke, "My Childhood vs. My Kids': 10 Big Changes," Mom.com, October 12, 2015, https://mom.com/momlife/23787-10-ways-my-kids-childhoods-are-different-my-own.

247. *2018 Grandparents Today National Survey: General Population Report* (Washington, DC: American Association of Retired Persons, 2019), www.aarp.org/content/dam/aarp/research/surveys_statistics/life-leisure/2019/aarp-grandparenting-study.doi.10.26419-2Fres.00289.001.pdf.

248. Nir Eyal, "Stanford Psychology Expert: This Is the No. 1 Skill Parents Need to Teach Their Kids—But Most Don't," September 10, 2019, CNBC, www.cnbc.com/2019/09/10/stanford-psychology-expert-biggest-parenting-mistake-is-not-teaching-kids-this-important-skill.html.

249. Sheila Quirke, "My Childhood vs. My Kids': 10 Big Changes," Mom.com, October 12, 2015, https://mom.com/momlife/23787-10-ways-my-kids-childhoods-are-different-my-own.

250. Daniel J. Cox, Jacqueline Clemence, and Eleanor O'Neil, 2019, *The Decline of Religion in American Family Life: Findings from the November 2019 American Perspectives Survey*, American Enterprise Institute, www.aei.org/research-products/report/the-decline-of-religion-in-american-family-life.

251. Kirsten Cole and Diandra Verwayne, "Becoming Upended: Teaching and Learning about Race and Racism with Young Children and Their Families," National Association for the Education of Young Children, May 2018, www.naeyc.org/resources/pubs/yc/may2018/teaching-learning-race-and-racism.

252. Some influential works include: Louise Derman-Sparks and Julie Olsen Edwards, *Anti-Bias Education for Young Children and Ourselves* (Washington, DC National Association for the Education of Young Children, 2009 and 2020); Louise Derman-Sparks and Patricia G. Ramsey: *What If All the Kids Are White? Anti-Bias Multicultural Education with Young Children and Families,* 2nd ed (New York: Teachers College Press, 2011); Louise Derman-Sparks, John Nimmo, and Debbie Leekeenan, *Leading Anti-Bias Early Childhood Programs: A Guide for Change* (New York: Teachers College Press, 2015).

253. Gitika Ahuja, "What a Doll Tells Us About Race," ABC News, March 31, 2009, https://abcnews.go.com/GMA/story?id=7213714&page=1.

254. Clark McKown and Michael J. Strambler, "Developmental Antecedents and Social and Academic Consequences of Stereotype-Consciousness in Middle Childhood," *Child Development* 80 (2009): 1643–1659, doi:10.1111/j.1467-8624.2009.01359.x.

255. Peter R. Blake et al., "The Ontogeny of Fairness in Seven Societies." *Nature* 528 (2015): 258–261.

256. Nathaniel K. Jones, "Learning about Racism: A Star Wars Story," *AAP Voices Blog,* American Academy of Pediatrics, July 29, 2019, www.aap.org/en-us/aap-voices/Pages/Learning-About-Racism.aspx.

257. Oprah Winfrey, "Oprah Winfrey Explores Revolutionary Approach to Childhood Trauma for '60 Minutes,'" United Way of Greater Philadelphia and Southern New Jersey, March 7, 2018, www.unitedforimpact.org/news/oprah-winfrey-explores-revolutionary-approach-to-childhood-trauma-for-60-minutes.

258. Katie A. Paciga and Chip Donohue, *Technology and Interactive Media for Young Children* (Latrobe, PA: Fred Rogers Center for Early Learning & Children's Media at Saint Vincent College and Chicago: Children's Media and Erickson Institute, 2017), http://www.fredrogerscenter.org/wp-content/uploads/2017/07/Technology-and-Interactive-Media-for-Young-Children.pdf.

259. Chip Donohue, "Tech in the Early Years: What Do We Know and Why Does It Matter?" Fred Rogers Center for Early Learning & Children's Media at Saint Vincent College, October 21, 2014, www.fredrogerscenter.org/2014/10/tech-in-the-early-years-what-do-we-know-and-why-does-it-matter.

260. T. Berry Brazelton, *Touchpoints: The Essential Reference—Your Child's Emotional and Behavioral Development* (Boston: Addison-Wesley Publishing Company, 1992).

261. To get started, look at the website of Zero to Three: www.zerotothree.org.

262. "Can Early Childhood Interventions Improve Health and Well-Being?" *Health Policy Snapshot Series,* Robert Wood Johnson Foundation, March 1, 2016, https://www.rwjf.org/en/library/research/2016/03/can-early-childhood-interventions-improve-life-outcomes-.html.

263. John Watson, *Psychological Care of Infant and Child* (New York: W. W. Norton & Company, 1928).

264. Michele Miller-Cox, "In the Rush to Improve Early Education, Don't Forget about Teachers," September 21, 2018, *Education Week,* www.edweek.org/ew/articles/2018/09/26/in-the-rush-to-improve-early-education.html.

265. Valora Washington and Brenda Gadson, *Guiding Principles for The New Early Childhood Professional: Building on Strength and Competence* (New York: Teachers College Press, 2017).

266. Franklin D. Roosevelt, "Address at the University of Pennsylvania, September 20, 1940," The Roosevelt Scholars, The Franklin Delano Roosevelt Foundation, https://fdrfoundation.org/the-roosevelt-scholars-program.

INDEX

academic development
  achievement gaps between racial
    groups, 87–88, 89
  discipline gaps and, 91, 92
  history of inequity, 88–89
  international comparisons of
    achievement, 83
  poverty and, 83, 87, 89, 97
  racial stereotypes and, 91–92
  role of family, 89, 97
  teaching and learning resources and,
    91–92
Adams, James Truslow, 52
adults, Alphas as, 37–38
advocacy for Alphas
  as act of justice, 95
  being bold in, 116–117
  children's inability to promote own
    interests, 66–67
  by government officials, 123
  hope and, 132, 133
  igniting, 120
  multigenerational agents for, 100–111
  need to act now, 9
  strategies for, 102–103
  "Strolling Thunder" event, 120–121
  uncertainties and transformation,
    121–124
aggression and technology, 32
AI (artificial intelligence)
  Alphas' interactions with, 31, 138
  effects of value of humans of, 40–41
Alpha Generation
  defined, xi
  generational cohorts of, 24–26
alternative futures planning, 106–107
Amazon moms, 58
Amel, Kate, 111
American Academy of Pediatrics, 31
American Association of Retired Persons
  (AARP), 132, 136

American Dream
  Americans' belief in, 127, 129
  Black population and, 55
  bootstrapping and self-made man in,
    51
  described, 51
  economic mobility as essential to,
    54–55
  as multigenerational accomplishment,
    122
  optimism as driving force, 126–127
  power of, 52
  social structures necessary for, 51, 52
American exceptionalism, 34, 107–109
American Institutes for Research, 69
Andrews, J. D., 9
Angelou, Maya, 12
Annie E. Casey Foundation, 7, 84–85
archetype, defined, 113
Asian population
  demographics, 3, 4
  family composition, 28
  immigration and growth in US of,
    35–36

behavior, race and assessments of
  children's, 7
Bennis, Warren, 120
Black population
  academic achievement, 87–88, 89
  acknowledgment of multiracial
    ancestry and, 38
  American Dream and, 55
  children in gifted programs, 92
  demographics, 36
  impact of coronavirus on, 21–22
  infant mortality rate, 86
  optimism about the future and, 130
  poverty rates, 87
  Race for Results Index scores, 85
  stereotypes and discipline in school,
    91, 92
  See also racial and ethnic minorities
Blake, Peter, 143
Boomers, problems left to future
  generations by, 25–26

bootstrapping
  as paradigm of American Dream, 51
  people of color and, 51
  as stress inducing, 56
Brandon, Richard, 112
Brazelton, T. Berry, 145
Brookings Institution, 16
Brown, Brené, 79
Brown v. Board of Education of Topeka
  (1954), 88

Canada, 55
Carney, Maria T., 57
Castro, Julian, 122
Center for American Progress, 71
challenges and American character, 127
change agents, 100–111
Child and Dependent Care Tax Credit
  (CDCTC), 72
child care (nonparental)
  affordability of, 71–72, 112
  ah hoc arrangements for, 71
  Amazon and, 58
  areas without licensed, 71
  belief that, weakens families, 67
  current state of, 46
  employment of women and, 57–59, 67
  generational beliefs in, 67–68
  infrastructure, 74
  as norm, 64
  productivity losses due to lack of, 57
  in US compared to OECD nations, 56
  See also early childhood education;
    universal free early childhood
    education
children
  ability to reduce poverty rates of, in
    US, 84
  access to child care for infants and
    toddlers, 71
  annual spending levels on, 85
  demographic shifts of, in cities and
    states, 36
  development during first one thousand
    days of life, 85, 112, 113
  development of growth mindset in,
    52–53
  failure of American, to meet
    development benchmarks, 7
  inability of, to promote and vote for
    own interests, 66–67
  increase in mixed-race and, of color,
    3, 35
  infant mortality, 83, 85–86
  intelligence and cognitive development
    of, valued by parents, 81–82
  multiplier effects of factors and benefits
    for, 95
  as nation's greatest asset, 2
  parental beliefs about supervision of,
    44–45
  percent of total parental income spent
    on, 27
  as percent of total population, 27, 33
  poverty and development of, 60
  poverty rates, 83, 84
  racial stereotypes and discipline in
    school, 91, 92
  room for growth on Race for Results
    Index scores, 85
  structured activities and, 45
  treatment of non-White in past and
    present, 5
The Children of 2010 (Washington and
  Andrews), 9
The Children of 2020 (Washington and
  Andrews), 9
The Children's Cause (Steiner), 102
Clinton, Bill, 132
Coates, Ta-Nehisi, 51
cognitive development
  amount of, before entering school,
    112, 113
  boosting brain development, 145–147
  poverty and, 83, 146
  social-emotional development and,
    144–145
  valued by parents, 81–82
cognitive dissonance, 109–110
"cognitive labor," 59
cohabitation of unmarried adults, 29
Coleman, James S., 88–89, 90, 97
color. *See* race; racial and ethnic
  minorities
commitment, need for, 151
community dynamics, 95–96
Comprehensive Child Development Act,
  67

confidence, need for, 150

coronavirus pandemic, 21–22, 150

courage
    as essential, 12–13
    existential life changes and, 14–16
    need for, 150
    original definition of, 79
    talking about changing racial
        populations and, 16–17
    uncertainty about promoting
        dispositions needed by Alphas and,
        13

Curran, Chris, 92

Daminger, Allison, 59

Danziger, Sheldon, 83

de Blasio, Bill, 123

demographic shifts
    in cities and states, 36
    now and in future, 3–4
    in past, 5

Derman-Sparks, Louise, 140–141, 143

de Tocqueville, Alexis, 117, 126

DiAngelo, Robin, 13, 17, 18

digital divide, 93–94

discomfort, working through, 113

disruptive innovators, 111

diversity
    actively teaching about, 138–139,
        142–143
    children's awareness of race, bias, and
        stereotypes, 139, 140–141
    defined, 19
    as new normal, 35–36
    public opinion about, 130–131, 132

Douglass, Frederick, 53

Downey, Douglas, 55

dual-language learners and early
    childhood education benefits, 65

DuBois, W. E. B., 38

Duggan, Mike, 123

*The Early Advantage 2—Building
    Systems That Work for Young Children:
    International Advantage 2—Building
    Systems That Work for Young Children*
    (Kagan), 69

early childhood education
    access problems, 70–71
    basic facts about, 10–11
    benchmarks of quality programs, 73
    benefits, 16, 64–65, 144, 146–147
    children's development of growth
        mindset and, 52–53
    components contributing to, 69
    early approaches, ix–x
    equity and investment in, 149
    "fix-it" approach, 64
    funding of, 89, 117
    government officials advocating for,
        123
    Head Start, 97
    importance of strong teacher-child
        interactions, 147
    labels for, 10
    as national economic asset, 65
    need for, x, 64
    professional staff issues, 14–16, 73–75,
        149
    professional staff standards, 45, 74
    quality of, 11, 72–73
    US enrollment rate compared to other
        OECD nations, 69
    See also child care; universal free early
        childhood education

Early Childhood Workforce Index, 75

economic mobility
    belief in importance of hard work for,
        127
    effect of education on, 93
    as essential to American Dream, 54–55
    in US and peer nations, 55

economic security
    competition across generations and, 25
    entrepreneurial and freelancing skills as
        necessary for, 40
    of families and employment of women,
        58, 59
    family size and, 27
    global conditions, 34
    skilling, reskilling, and upskilling as
        necessary for, 39, 40

economy of US
    ability to reduce childhood poverty, 84
    annual per child spending levels, 85
    benefits of early childhood education
        to, 16, 65
    portion of GDP spent on social
        programs, 84
    productivity losses due to lack of child
        care, 57
    value of invisible labor, 59
EdBuild, 92
education
    lifelong learning, 39–41
    opportunity equity and, 64–65, 87–92
    optimism about the future and level
        of, 130
    reinvention of traditional, 38–39
    See also early childhood education
elders, need to support increasing number
    of, 41, 57
equality, defined, 19
Equality of Educational Opportunity
    (Coleman), 88–89, 90, 97
equity
    as core issue, 70, 149
    defined, 19
    See also opportunity equity
equity lens, 121
ethnic minorities. *See* racial and ethnic
    minorities
Every Student Succeeds Act (ESSA,
    2015), 89
explicit biases, defined, 19

families
    belief that nonparental child care
        weakens, 67
    employment of women and economic
        security of, 58, 59
    empowerment of, 100–102
    grandparents, 136
    paid leave for, 55, 59–60, 78
    public support for funding policies
        supporting, 117
    role in academic achievement of, 89,
        97
    self-sufficiency/self-reliance myth, 66
    size and economic security, 27

social-emotional competence role of,
    145, 146
structure of
    future, 28–29
    multiple changes in, 135–136
    nuclear, 64
    one-child, 26, 27
    racial and ethnic minorities and, 28
    single-parent, 29, 87
    "two-generation model" programs and,
        97, 98
    UBI or child benefits for, 60–61
    See also parents and parenting
Family Medical Leave Act (US), 55
Fell, Ashley, 32, 37
Ferguson, Ronald, 91
Fisher, Benjamin, 92
Fixed Nation and Fluid Nation scenarios
    described, 2, 8
    overview of, 118–119
    transformative game changers and, 48,
        113–116
Frey, William H., 3, 36
the future
    ability to invent, 2–3, 6
    Americans' optimism about, 126–127,
        130
    being bold about, 107–109, 116–117
    consideration of multiple possible,
        111–112
    decision-making approaches to,
        113–116
    multigenerational change agents,
        100–111
    possible scenarios, 2
    racial and ethnic minorities most
        optimistic about, 135
    scenario planning for, 106–107, 108
    validating cognitive dissonance and
        Americans' lived experiences,
        109–110
    See also Fixed Nation and Fluid Nation
        scenarios

Gabor, Dennis, 2
Gadson, Brenda, 111, 149

game changers
  defined, 47
  hope and, 132
  overview of, 6–7
  preservation of perennial strengths and,
    149
  See also transformative game changers
Gandhi, Mahatma, 6
Gardella, Joseph, 92
Garfinkel, Irwin, 97
Generation Alpha
  current birth rate, 23
  names for, 31
  population projections for 2050, 23
  term coined, 22
*A Generation of Sociopaths:How the Baby
  Boomers Betrayed America* (Gibney),
  25–26
Gibney, Bruce Cannon, 25–26
Gibran, Kahlil, 126
gifted programs, 92
Glass, Jennifer, 54
global connections, 33–35
"Global Trends 2030: Worlds" (National
  Intelligence Council), 1
GoDaddy, 29–30
Goffin, Stacie, 112, 113
Grasso, David, 129–130
Green, Holly, 107
Grissom, Jason A., 92
Gross-Loh, Christine, 56
growth mindset, 52–53
*Guiding Principles for the New Early
  Childhood Educator* (Washington and
  Gadson), 149

Hall, Granville Stanley, 27
Hammond, Linda Darling, 92, 93
Handy, Charles, 126–127
Hanushek, Eric, 95
happiness, 128–129
Harari, Yuval Noah, 35, 40–41
Harkness, Sara, 81–82
Haskins, Ron, 54–55, 97
Haspel, Elliot, 112
Head Start, 97
Heckman, James, 65, 113
"The Hispanic paradox," 86

Hispanic population
  academic achievement, 87–88, 89
  children in gifted programs, 92
  demographics, 3, 4, 36
  family composition, 28
  immigration and growth in US of,
    35–36
  infant mortality rate, 86
  optimism about the future and, 130
  poverty and, 5, 87
  Race for Results Index scores, 85
  racial identity and, 38
history, effect of demographic shifts, 5
hope
  advocacy and, 132, 133
  as bedrock of America, 128, 133
  deficit of, 128
  game changers and, 132
  need to concentrate on, 134
  in Pandora's box, 17, 131
  See also optimism
Huggins, Ericka, 79

Ikeda, Daisaku, 2
imagination, need for, 151
immigration, growth in Asian and
  Hispanic population in US, 35–36
implicit bias, defined, 19
inclusion, defined, 19
income inequality, 129
infant mortality, 83, 85–86
Institute of Electrical and Electronics
  Engineers (IEEE), 30
intelligence, valued by parents, 81–82
invisible labor, 59
Issacs, Julia, 54–55

John Dickinson, 110
John XXIII (pope), 134
Jones, Nathaniel K., 142
Jung, Carl, 113

Kagan, Sharon Lynn, 69, 83–84
Kennedy, John, 127
Kerner Commission report, 88
King, Martin Luther, Jr., 79, 95
Kuhn, Thomas, 63–64, 95

Levin, Diane, 31

life expectancy, 24, 56, 57
Lincoln, Abraham, 82
Lord, Anton, 30

Mandela, Nelson, 2
Mann, Horace, 93
math skills and social class, 7
McAuliff, Katherine, 143
McCrindle, Mark, 22, 37
McGrady, Patrick B., 7
McLanahan, Sara, 97
Mead, Margaret, 64, 126
megatrends
  demographic shift, 3–4
  inevitable, 20, 21–22
  overview of, 19
  transformative game changers and, 2
meritocracy, 51–52
microaggression, defined, 117
Millennials
  economic worries of, 25
  as parents, 14, 30
Miller-Cox, Michele, 147
Mistral, Gabriela, 9
"Mother's Pensions," 67
multiculturalism. *See* diversity

National Academy of Sciences, 84
National Association for the Education of
  Young Children, 16
National Center for Health Research, 32
National Institute for Early Education
  Research, 73, 95
National Intelligence Council, 1
National Public Radio poll, 129
National Recreation and Park
  Association, 44
*The New Early Childhood Professional:
  A Step-by-Step Guide to Overcoming
  Goliath* (Washington, Gadson, and
  Amel), 111
Newman, Susan, 27
Newsom, Gavin, 123
New York Times, 94
Nixon, Richard, 67
No Child Left Behind Act (NCLB,
  2002), 89
nuclear family, 64

Obama, Barack, 18, 82, 128
OECD (Organization for Economic Co-
  operation and Development)
  child care, 56
  paid family leave, 55
  US enrollment rate compared to other
    OECD nations, 69
Ogilvy, Jay, 108
Oncken, Lindsay, 72
opportunity equity
  achievement of
    not possible with currents systems
      and methods, 96–97
    strategies for, 95, 96, 98–102
    time of, at current pace of growth,
      95
  basic cornerstones of, 82–84
  as basic to free society, 82
  digital divide and, 93–94
  education and, 64–65, 87–92
  empowerment of families and,
    100–102
  health and, 83, 85–86
  overview, 80
optimism
  of Black population about the future,
    130
  decrease in, 129
  as driving force of American Dream,
    126–127
  education and, 130
  racial and ethnic minorities having
    most, about the future, 135
  See also hope

paid family leave policies, 55, 59–60, 78
Pandora's box, 17, 131
paradigm shift concept, 63–64, 95
parents and parenting
  beliefs about quality of their child care,
    73
  beliefs about supervision of children,
    44–45
  characteristics of Alphas', 28
  child care as responsibility of one,
    67–68
  childhood of, compared to Alphas',
    135–137

happiness of, in US and peer nations, 53, 54

helicopter, 45

importance of, x

influences on buying decisions, 32, 33

intelligence and cognitive development of children valued by, 81–82

invisible labor of, 59

involvement approaches to achieve opportunity equity, 98–99

maximum feasible participation by, 97

need to organize for advocacy, 103

paid family leave, 55, 59–60, 78

percent of total income spent on children, 27

poverty rates of single-, 87

stressed-out, multitasking lives of, 43–44, 56

support systems for, 52, 54

transmission of culture and values through, 142–143

See also families

Pearman, Francis A., II, 92

Pelecas, Sapphiroula, 30

Pew Research Center

belief in American exceptionalism, 34, 108–109

generational beliefs in child care, 67–68

impact of diversity, 130–131

parental beliefs about supervision of children, 44–45

structure of future families, 28, 29

play, 31, 44

Polis, Jared, 123

population

children as percent of total, 27, 33

growth of children of color, 35

projections, 23, 37, 130

poverty

ability to reduce childhood rates of, in US, 84

in Canada, 55

child development and academic achievement and, 60, 83, 87, 89, 97, 146

early childhood education benefits and, 64–65

generational, 134

problems accessing child care and, 71

racial and ethnic minorities and, 86–87

tolerance of, in US, 83

public resources and modern life, 64

Quirke, Sheila, 136

race

assessments of children's behavior and, 7

meaning of, to Alphas, 37, 38

as problem of twentieth century, 38

reluctance to talk about, 17

Race for Results Index (Annie E. Casey Foundation), 84–85

racial and ethnic minorities

academic achievement of, 87–88, 89

children in gifted programs, 92

demographic shift and, 1, 3–4

educational funding and, 91–92

educational segregation, 88, 90–91

as engines of America's future growth, 35–36

family composition, 28

infant mortality rates, 83, 85–86

as majority of American population (2050), 130

optimism about the future and, 130, 135

poverty and, 5, 86–87

pride in heritages, 37

problems accessing child care, 71

Race for Results Index scores, 84–85

universal free child care and, 67

reading skills and social class, 7

Real Clear Politics poll, 129

Redding, Christopher, 93

Reiner, Rob, 103

restorative justice, 19

Reynolds, John R., 7
Riley, Naomi Schaefer, 94
The Rise of the Meritocracy (Young), 51–52
risk assessment and technology, 32
Robert Woods Johnson Foundation, 146
Rogers, Fred, 144
Rogers, Luke, 3
Roosevelt, Franklin Delano, 133, 151

Sawhill, Isabel, 54–55, 92
scenario planning for the future,
    106–107, 108
Schieder, Jessica, 84, 87
Schieller, Ben, 26
segregation, 88, 90–91
self-made man
    as fallacious, 53, 54–55, 109–110
    megatrends and, 46
    as paradigm of American Dream, 51
self-sufficiency/self-reliance myth, 66
Sengupta, Somini, 34
"serve and return" interactions, 145
Shierholz, Heidi, 57
single parent families, 29
sleep and technology, 32
social class and reading and math skills, 7
social-emotional development, 144–145,
    146
social generations, characteristics of,
    22–23
social infrastructure, 39
specialization, 39–40
Statista, 26
Steiner, Gil, 102
"Strolling Thunder" event, 120–121
Super, Charles M., 81–82

technology
    advocacy for Alphas and, 120
    constantly changing, 143
    creative play and, 31
    digital divide, 93–94
    negative effects of, on Alphas, 32
    role of, in lives of Alphas, 29–31, 44,
        143–144
Ton-Quinlivan, Van, 39

transformative game changers
    effects of, 46–47, 48
    meeting and accepting, 148
    megatrends and, 2
    need for, 134
    overview, 45–46
    See also universal systems for
        supporting people
Trump, Donald, 59–60
Turkington, Eric, 32–33
"two-generation model" programs, 97, 98
Tyrrell, Ian, 34

United Nations Convention on the
    Rights of the Child, 103
universal basic income (UBI), 60–61, 63
universal free early childhood education
    barriers to, 65–68
    cultural mythologies opposing, 66,
        67–68
    nations with, 69
    overview of, 62, 76–77
    strategies to achieve, 77–79
universal systems for supporting people
    happiness of parents and, 54
    life expectancy and, 56
    as necessary for American Dream to
        continue, 52
    overview of, 50
    paid family leave, 55, 59–60, 78
    in peer nations, 54
    strategies to achieve, 59–61
    women in workforce and, 57–59
University of Texas, 53
US Department of Health and Human
    Services, 57, 71

voice assistants and Alphas, 31, 32–33

wages, of early childhood educators,
    15–16
Walsh, Martin J., 123
Washington, Valora, 9, 111, 149
Watson, John, 146
white fragility, 17, 18
*White Fragility: Why It's So Hard for White
    People to Talk about Racism* (DiAngelo),
    17